千万里路

Sweet Mandarin

始于一步

千万里路 始于一步

Sweet Mandarin

Helen Tse

EBURY
PRESS

1 3 5 7 9 10 8 6 4 2

Published in 2007 by Ebury Press, an imprint of Ebury Publishing

Ebury Publishing is a division of the Random House Group

Copyright © Helen Tse 2007

Helen Tse has asserted her right to be identified as the author of this Work in accordance with the Copyright, Designs and Patents Act 1988

The Random House Group Limited Reg. No. 954009

Addresses for companies within the Random House Group can be found at www.randomhouse.co.uk

A CIP catalogue record for this book is available from the British Library

The Random House Group Limited makes every effort to ensure that the papers used in our books are made from trees that have been legally sourced from well-managed and credibly certified forests. Our paper procurement policy can be found on www.randomhouse.co.uk

Typeset by e-type, Liverpool
Printed and bound in Great Britain by Mackays of Chatham Ltd

Hardback ISBN 9780091913618
Export trade paperback ISBN 9780091920197

Contents

Preface

'To the ruler, the people are Heaven; to the people, food is Heaven'
君以民为天 民以食为天。

My grandmother Lily Kwok was born in a small village in Southern China in 1918, confounding the midwife who'd predicted that she must be a boy because she had kicked so hard in the womb. That independence, strength and energy stayed with her all her life. Lily is 88 now, and still a fit, intelligent and – I'm afraid to say – stubborn woman despite all that she has been through. She and I are very alike. Lily and my mother, Mabel, inspired and shaped much of what I have done with my life: my success at school and in business; my return to the catering trade; my journey back to China to rediscover my roots, and in doing so, discovering her roots too. Her story is my story, and it's the story of Sweet Mandarin.

My sisters and I were immersed from birth in the Chinese catering business – the fourth generation of our family to make a living from food. We grew up in a family firm that was built on decades of graft and hard-earned experience, and we were expected to give up our evenings and weekends to help out behind the counter or in the kitchen. Not surprisingly, by the time we were teenagers we just wanted a way out. I became a lawyer, Lisa, my twin, a financier and Janet an engineer, but for all our efforts to escape we found ourselves choosing to follow in Mabel and Lily's footsteps in the end. We opened our own restaurant together in 2004, and called it Sweet Mandarin.

None of our friends in the Manchester Chinese community understood why we were doing it. The restaurant business is a very demanding one – the hours are long, the work hard and the economics precarious. One moment you're in the black, the next something unexpected has plunged you into the red. It's a tough, male-dominated world too, so why would three twenty-something professional ladies with good degrees and white-collar careers want to risk it all for something they'd seen their parents slave over all their lives?

Our friends in Manchester had done everything they could to avoid taking on any responsibility for their own parents' restaurants and takeaways, even moving hundreds of miles away so it was impossible for their family to call them up and expect them to rush home to help out. Living any nearer would involve a burden of guilt and obligation from which they were desperate to be free. I could count on one hand the number of my Chinese peers who were going back into catering.

They thought we were taking a step backwards, and even at the huge street party we held for the restaurant's launch, with fire-crackers and performers and champagne, I could see them quietly shaking their heads over the choice we'd made. The generation

above them understood though. I remember old Chinese – the
bosses of the established Chinatown restaurants and supermarkets
– smiling on us with respect. It was an acknowledgement that we
were carrying the flickering, dimming torch for a new generation,
and they wished their own sons and daughters would do the same,
keeping the community alive and handing down traditional recipes
and family business know-how to their own children.

Opening my own restaurant gave me all those things; it was
much, much more than a chance to test my entrepreneurial streak.
It brought me closer to my sisters, for a start, and though I'm the
voice for all of us in this book, they share this heritage with me as
well as the work of setting up Sweet Mandarin. It also introduced
me to my grandmother and mother all over again and opened up a
bridge between us that crossed East and West, uniting the present
and the past. I came to understand what their lives had been, and
what my generation represented to them.

Lisa, Janet and I had problems getting our business off the
ground, but all our slog and late nights were nothing compared to
Mabel and Lily's struggle. They arrived in Britain from Hong Kong
with nothing, strangers in a foreign country. Everything they had
they built from sheer perseverance and toil, and everything we had
came from them.

Every Saturday morning, my mother, grandmother and I shop
at the Chinese supermarket. We buy stock for the kitchens at Sweet
Mandarin and food for our own home cooking. In the past I'd only
known the barest facts about my grandmother's long life, but when
we began these weekly trips she started to reveal the real story, bit

by bit. I'd known some things already – just the anecdotes and the funny characters that make up family folklore – but now the detail and the scale of what my grandmother had gone through began to emerge. It was as though each bottle or package that she picked out for our basket was tied to a different chapter of her life, and now she wanted to share it with us. When your entire family works in restaurants, food becomes a family album – an heirloom that triggers memories.

Very little has been written about the experiences of mainland Chinese immigrants to Hong Kong and to Britain, but I knew that as I discovered more about the journey my grandmother had made, and the extraordinary things that had happened to her, this was a story that had to be told. It's shared by many of the Chinese who settled in this country, who also carved out a place in their new homeland through the catering trade.

It's a story that will be familiar to immigrants all over the world – and not just those from China – those who leave their place of birth behind to build a home in a new country, often struggling to survive. My story is about my grandmother, my mother and myself: three generations of independent Chinese women whose lives take in Guangzhou in southern China in the 1920s, colonial Hong Kong in the 1930s, the horrors of the Japanese occupation and a changing England from the 1950s to the present day. Like all families, we've been caught up in the times we lived in, shaken by the unpredictable and devastating upheavals in the Far East in the twentieth century, but the women in my family have always come through and lived to tell their tales.

There is no other book that can tell this story because no one else has walked in our shoes. Like the Chinese cooking which has saved us, my family fortunes contain layers of meaning and wisdom that cannot be easily explained. This is a book that is written from the heart and which seeks to remember past generations with gratitude and thanks; it is both a witness to the kindness and cruelty of people and a demonstration of how resilient human beings can be. Sometimes it seems as if the most terrible of times have brought out the best in my family.

I offer you this book in the spirit of Lily Kwok's Chicken Curry, Mabel's Claypot and Buddha's Golden Picnic Basket, and in honour of the exceptional women who gave me a chance in the world.

Gambei – Cheers!

Helen Tse

Chapter One

THE LITTLE SACK OF RICE
GUANGZHOU, CHINA 1918–1925

'The journey of a thousand miles starts with one step'

千万里路始于一步

My grandmother Lily grew up in a small farming village close to the city of Guangzhou, a port on the Pearl River in south eastern China. Downstream of the city, the Pearl splits into a vast delta and spills into the South China Sea, and on either side of its mouth lie the prosperous old colonies of Hong Kong and Macau. Guangzhou has always been called 'the Flower City' because it has warm, wet, monsoon weather which means that, unusually for China, flowers bloom there all year round.

According to local folktales, the fields of flowers which surrounded the city first blossomed when five celestial deities rode in on five rams, each with an ear of rice in its mouth. The immortals gave the rice ears to the farmers and promised them that there would never be famine in Guangzhou. When they flew away, they left behind the rams who turned into stone and became the sculptures which now sit in Yuexiu Park in the city. The legend is beautiful, and promises prosperity, but when my grandmother was born in the region in 1918 she only knew extreme poverty.

When I was a teenager my grandmother and I would spend hours watching her favourite Chinese language soap operas together. I could barely understand a word the actors said and the simple plots wound on endlessly, but the folk-story style was easy enough for me to follow, and every week we tuned in eagerly to get our fix of melodrama. One storyline came up again and again: an evil landlord would turf out a young woman and her child when she fell behind with the rent and rejected his amorous advances. She would then cry a lot, before being rescued by a handsome kung fu fighter, who arrived in the village with a flourish. Naively, I once asked my grandmother if that was what it was really like in the pre-revolutionary China she had known. 'If only,' she sighed, shaking her head.

She didn't make much of the deprivation she'd known as a child, but I knew that unlike me, she'd never taken the comfort of a warm bed and a well-stocked kitchen for granted. Her China was still recovering from its catastrophic losses in World War One when the 1918–19 Spanish Flu pandemic struck, killing over 20 million people – even more lives were lost than in the war itself. Piles of corpses littered China's vast plains.

Her father, Leung, and her mother, Tai Po, were betrothed to each other long before the war broke out. The marriage wasn't founded on romance, but a contract formulated by their parents, and they were only four years old when the match was made. Their engagement followed a strict set of practices dictated by a Chinese tradition called 'Three Letters and Six Etiquettes' which marked the progress of their union from match to marriage, and all families, rich or poor, observed these stages which had been laid down over two and a half thousand years previously during the Warring States period of Chinese history.

The most important of the six etiquettes came first. Leung's parents singled out Tai Po as a suitable daughter-in-law by hiring an astrologer to make calculations based on the date and place of her birth; they then dispatched a matchmaker to formally propose to the newborn girl's parents. Tai Po and Leung grew up knowing about their engagement, and even met a few times. Each of the etiquettes was marked by a ceremonial performance or a formal letter.

The 'Gift Letter' detailed an inventory of goods that formed a kind of inverse dowry, sent by the groom's parents to the bride, rather than vice versa. To Tai Po, who was all of 11 and had nothing to call her own, it must have seemed like a dazzling array. Parcels of teas and spices, lotus seeds, baskets of fruit and red and green beans, bottles of wine, spindles of hair ribbon, bridal cakes and packages of delicacies were showered on her. Who knows whether she could have fully understood the implications of accepting them, but she wouldn't have had much choice in the matter.

When she was 14 an astrologer was consulted once more to work out an auspicious date for the wedding, which was set for a year later. A final letter was presented on the day of the wedding ceremony itself, and confirmed and commemorated the formal acceptance of Tai Po into my great-grandfather Leung's family.

In today's China people marry whom they choose for love, but my great-grandparents were as good as strangers on their wedding day. That morning Tai Po would have been dressed by her mother and sisters in red – for luck and good fortune – before being taken to the groom's home for the ceremony. She never went back – from that day on, Tai Po belonged to Leung and his family by both civil and religious law.

I'm told Leung was terrified by the formal rituals and cried throughout the proceedings, and though my great-grandmother was no older than him, she comforted and tried to reassure him. Her family wasn't wealthy and she brought barely anything with her to the marriage other than a few handmade kitchen utensils and some sticks of furniture; in keeping with tradition the new couple moved into Leung's parents' house, where they were expected to behave according to a strict code of propriety.

They were forbidden to show any overt affection for one another, and Tai Po's duty was to obey and serve her mother-in-law. She did the housework and she worked in the fields of the family farm, but her most important task was producing a male heir for the family – everything else was secondary. Leung and Tai Po were lucky that although their marriage was arranged they got on well despite the pressures they faced from Leung's clan.

As they worked and lived side by side they developed a mutual respect which soon deepened into love. As daughter-in-law, Tai Po had the lowest status in the household, and Leung was bound to defer to his parents always, but he managed to be a supportive, caring husband who stood by her through hard times. They were hard times, too. My great-grandmother gave birth to and lost three sons, none of whom survived beyond their second birthday, and although in the end she gave Leung six children who survived to adulthood, they were all girls.

Some of my grandmother's first memories are of her brothers' deaths. She remembers the eldest sleeping in his cot one night, and then, the next day when he did not wake, the way that her mother screamed. A dark cloud fell on the house. For months her parents were tearful and solemn; no one in the family was allowed to speak about what had happened.

The villagers viewed the deaths with superstition, and some began to suggest that Leung's family was cursed. When her third son died, Tai Po demanded that they move to another house, thinking that the very ground on which their shack stood must have been cursed by an evil spirit, but no one would buy it – everyone knew about the baby boys and was afraid that they too would be jinxed if they bought the house.

It's difficult for twenty-first century Westerners to grasp how big a blow it was for my great-grandfather to lose those baby boys one by one. In Chinese families, even today, boys are treated like kings. I'm one of four – three girls, and a boy who was born last and to a real fanfare, even in our not-so traditional family. The whole household celebrated his birth for several days in grand style, toasting his future and congratulating themselves on having a male heir at last. It shows the influence of our home culture – the son is the one who will carry on the family business and look after the parents when they are too old to work. For my great-grandfather Leung to lose three sons was disastrous.

Leung's mother bullied Tai Po about her failure to produce an heir, stirring up trouble in the mourning household. It was cruel, but grounded in a real fear – China was a patrilineal society and Leung's six daughters were growing up with no rights over their own inheritance, so if there was no son, the family lost every entitlement to its own property, land and business. When my great-grandfather Leung died, everything he owned would be passed to his nearest male descendant – probably a nephew – leaving my grandmother and her sisters at the mercy of fate.

While Leung still lived the family bloodline continued, and when his parents died he and Tai Po came into sole possession of the house and the land around it. Its walls were made of dried, plastered mud and its roof was straw. There was only one room, which had a stone floor where the children played and where work was done during the day. At night, sleeping mats were rolled out, and each person found their narrow patch of floor.

The cramped conditions meant that the hut was infested with lice and other parasites which crawled over any bits of skin that poked out from under blankets and clothing. They crawled through the family's hair and bit into their scalps and ears, raising lumps. When they shook out the cloth sheets in the morning before folding them away, my grandmother told me you could hear the clicking noise of the insects hitting the stone floor, swollen and red with the blood they'd sucked.

The land around Guangzhou where the village stood didn't have the city's soft climate. No flower could bloom all year round there. The winters were long and bitterly cold, and Leung's girls were out in all weathers collecting grass and dried husks for the family fire. If there wasn't enough to keep the fire going, the temperature fell rapidly, and any other fuel was too expensive to contemplate.

The mud walls were inadequate and during the rainy season the house was both wet and cold, twisting Tai Po's joints with rheumatism. In summer it was hot and humid, and the family baked inside the little hut, so like the rest of the village, they preferred to sleep outside when the season was at its height.

When I travelled to Guangzhou in 2002 I stayed in a hotel that was housed in a skyscraper, flanked by a mall through which an endless parade of well-dressed and affluent shoppers paraded in the latest designer labels. The complex stood in the middle of a spaghetti junction of roads that were jammed with cars belching exhaust fumes. It seemed to me as though China had accelerated through several centuries' worth of change in just a few short decades; it would have been unrecognisable to Leung and Tai Po.

They were raising their family in a village that had followed the same patterns of agriculture and social customs for hundreds and hundreds of years. People grew their food in their own vegetable patches and paddy-fields. There were no medicines other than traditional remedies, and scant communication with the outside world. To be born a farmer meant to die as one, trapped in a cycle of poverty that was bequeathed to the next generation, and in order to survive famine, flooding and periodic attacks by bandits, everyone worked doggedly towards a common goal – feeding and clothing their families.

It was worse for women. That same patrilineal system of

inheritance condemned girls to be a burden – they were subhuman, their birth to be dreaded. Mao Tse Tung once wrote that all Chinese people had three ropes around their necks: political authority, clan authority and religious authority. He omitted to mention that a woman has a fourth: the authority of her husband.

It was engrained in the Chinese feudal social system long before Mao, when Confucius sanctioned the age-old domination of fathers over daughters and husbands over wives, incorporating it into the conservative values of Confucianism – with its emphasis on strong ethics, the importance of family and respect for elders, and above all a cold and logical approach to man's problems. Even at the beginning of the twentieth century Confucius was still the predominant influence on most Chinese people, and for thousands of years political power had gone hand in hand with the control and subjugation of women.

Not only did they have no rights over property or the work they put into a family's prosperity, but they couldn't count on having their voices heard when decisions were made which affected the family and wider clan. Education was certainly not an option, which was a great shame for my grandmother – an intelligent and inquisitive child – but the course of her life was set out at birth. She would be married to a man her parents chose, and she would be little more than his property, with no will of her own.

A Chinese saying sums it up: 'Having married a cock she must follow the cock; having married a dog she must follow the dog; having married a carrying pole she must carry it for life.' All that lay ahead of Lily was a life of discrimination, poverty and drudgery.

You could say she was lucky as the third girl born to a rural family – lucky that her parents weren't so desperate that they abandoned or murdered her to save the family's scarce resources. Every year in that period thousands of baby girls died simply because of their sex; they were poisoned, left exposed on the hillsides, suffocated or buried alive, and some mothers even believed that the sacrifice of a daughter guaranteed the birth of a son the following year. I can even imagine that they convinced themselves that sentencing their female offspring to death was better than condemning them to life as a woman in China, though it's hard to grasp the sheer wretchedness that would lead someone to believe that.

Leung was ahead of his time because he felt strongly that his daughters were valuable in their own right, and that even though they weren't the much longed for sons, they too would contribute to the all-important family tree. Their efforts might not bear fruit until a future generation, but they would not be wasted. My grandmother took this conviction, and her own natural self-belief and determination, and changed her destiny; in doing so, she changed the destiny of her daughters and their daughters in turn.

When I was at school I always knew that I wanted to become a lawyer, and my parents would worry that the law wasn't the right profession for a woman – it was a man's world, as far as they were concerned – but my grandmother only encouraged me. She told me a story that her father, Leung, often told her when she was a little girl, which summed up all he believed about the value of patience and a steadfast commitment to one's own ambitions whatever happened.

In the tale, an eccentric old man announces to his village that he will demolish two mountains so that he can run a road south to the Han river. His neighbour scoffs, 'That's ridiculous! How can one man dispose of so much earth and stones?' The old man replies simply, 'Though I shall die, I shall leave behind my son, and my son's son. From generation to generation I hand this task. Since these mountains cannot grow any larger, why shouldn't we be able to level them?' After five generations the mountains were finally flattened, and the road built.

That story stuck with her all her life. Her father always told her that even though she was a girl, she could earn her place in the world and leave a legacy for her own children and grand-children, just like the man in the story who moved the mountains. It was a valuable lesson, and as she lugged buckets of water, helped her mother in the shack or laboured in the fields day in and day out, that story must have become a mantra for her. As Leung struggled with poverty and poor harvests, his whole family worked together for their own survival, sowing, watering and harvesting the crops that would fill their bellies. Their clothes were simple, coarse cotton, and the tools they had were primitive and mended many times over, but they were bonded together knowing that they all depended on one another.

There was always a crowd of younger children in the village who were too small to help in the fields or be parcelled out to local factories, and as there was no school they were left pretty much to their own devices for a few years. At first Lily ran wild with the other girls and boys, getting into scrapes and earning a reputation for being a good-natured, if obstinate, little child.

She had fat cheeks which were made ruddy with cold by the sharp winter weather, and flat East Asian bones framing a fleshy little button of a nose and full, red lips. She wore her hair in little mismatched pigtails and had a wicked smile that revealed a row of tiny, rotten, milk teeth. She still has that grin, of pure mischief, despite her age. She was best-known for her eyes though, which were dark and piercing, and always curious. You always got the sense that she was trying to work something – or someone – out, and that her mind was whirring away.

To keep out the cold she wore a *meen lap*, or thick padded jacket made from deep red cotton, a hand-me-down from her elder sister. Somehow, Lily never seemed to grow into the coat, and was utterly dwarfed by it, which made the other villagers laugh. They affectionately called her 'sack of rice', and teased her mercilessly.

'What's that?' her father would joke as she waddled past in the red jacket, with only the tips of her fingers poking from the sleeves and the collar up to her ears, 'I've never seen a sack of rice that could carry itself. Somebody catch it and store it in the barn!' Then he'd chase a giggling Lily round the small yard, making her scream and laugh and beg him to stop.

There was no money for toys so the sisters played 'paper, scissors, stone' for hours at a time, lining up opposite one another and counting to three, before 'revealing' what they had in their clenched palms. My grandmother taught my mother, and my mother taught us 20 years later, and Janet, Lisa and I would play it on the back seat of the car as she drove us home from school. It kept us every bit as entertained as it had our grandmother in that far-away village.

The hamlet sat on a vast, open plain of land crossed by a series of small rivers, all of which led to the mighty Pearl River itself. There were about 30 huts of different sizes, some more sturdy than others, all backing on to a lake. At the back of each house was a set of steps which led straight down to the water's edge where the women of each family washed clothes and bedrolls. At one end of the village was a bridge that led to the road to Guangzhou, and every morning the peasants would gather there, hoping to catch a ride to the city to look for work.

Despite the privations of life in the village, the atmosphere was communal and lively. Everyone knew everyone else's business, and the few hundred residents were all related somehow, either by blood or by marriage. Leung's family lived next to the fish-pond, alongside the village pigpens. The pigs themselves were usually at liberty to roam around the small yards and root for food, and they were a great source of entertainment for the smaller children.

My grandmother and her sisters would dare each other to ride on the pigs in a pint-sized Chinese rodeo – whoever stayed on the furious animals longest won, and Lily still rocks with laughter when she tells me how hard it was. A fully grow pot-bellied pig is almost the same height as a little Chinese peasant girl, and the wiry hair on their backs is wickedly ticklish. The girls would have to chase the pigs then try to vault on to them as their friends raced behind, pulling the beasts' curly tails to make them buck and run faster.

The pigs were filthy and their riders always ended up being tossed into the mud, so at the end of the day the little 'sack of rice' would come home plastered from head to foot in dirt, stinking to high heaven. Tai Po wouldn't let her into the house, and would toss her into the fish-pond to wash off the worst – a quick dunk in the chilly water served as a scolding for Lily's naughtiness too, but I doubt it put her off the pig rodeo for long.

The huts didn't have kitchens, but kept their fires for warmth alone. Everyone in the village shared a cooking area next to the well, and as the women spent a good deal of their day there, it was a hotbed of news and gossip about all the goings-on.

There was a single clay kiln oven that was stoked with wood or coal and had two levels. The top was an open fire for boiling up soups, a staple of the peasant diet, eked out with barley, pieces of dried meat preserved with salt and broken bits of tofu. Ginger would be thrown into the pot too, to keep the body warm, kill off bacteria and add its distinctive tang to the otherwise plain broth.

The open fire was also used for cooking with large, round, iron pans called woks. The women fanned the cinders with bamboo bellows until the coals glowed red hot, and flames escaped that were large enough to lick all the way round the pan and sear the food that was frying, sealing in its flavour. This skill is called *wok-hey* or 'breath of the wok', and takes some mastering, but it makes the wok the most versatile of cooking tools. You could stir fry vegetables or braise a freshly caught fish whole, and the intoxicating smell of the food being skillfully turned this way and that by a savvy cook would spread through the village, drawing a hungry crowd.

Under the fire was an oven were the women baked soya beans and rice. When times were hard and stocks fell low, there was sweet potato to make up the shortfall. They grew in abundance on the small strips of land that weren't rich enough for the more valuable crops, and would be roasted in their own husks, giving off a whiff of toffee as they caramelised. Peel off the skin, and the pulp inside is cooked to a sweet, piping-hot mush – real comfort food, even if it didn't have much nutritional value.

I can imagine how good it must have tasted to the workers after a long, bitterly cold day on the fields; you would have gobbled it down quickly, burning your mouth, then felt it travel all the way down to your empty, rumbling stomach. Sweet potatoes kept hunger away when the villagers were desperate, but my grandmother also recalls that they made everyone fart atrociously, so perhaps that's one reason why they weren't popular – when a whole family shared one small room, flatulence was the last thing you wanted!

For most of the year their diet was bland and monotonous, stoked with bowls of sticky rice flavoured with salty soy sauce. Treats were few and far between, but families saved up to splash out on *lap cheong*, strings of dried and fatty pork sausages studded with greasy nubs, like a sort of sweet salami. They were reserved for Chinese New Year, when they were dished up on beds of fluffy white rice flavoured by the aromatic *lap cheong* juices. My grandmother still goes into raptures remembering this delicacy, and the way that she and her friends would suck every single grain of rice to relish every last particle of the succulent *lap cheong* grease.

Each family carried their food back from the cooking area to eat it at their own hut, perched on small stools with a bowl of rice in one hand and a set of chopsticks in the other. When Lily talks about the village of her childhood, it's the aroma of the food that she remembers first, snaking out from the great oven that glowed in the heart of the village, and down the small alleyways between the shacks, drawing the young girls home to their family and to supper.

It was a simple life, lived at subsistence level and its pleasures were simple too, despite the hardships. Days, weeks, months and years slowly passed by, and eventually Lily was old enough to be put to work herself. While the countryside had stagnated for centuries, the Industrial Revolution was now spreading out from the largest cities and beginning to transform lives in the nearby villages. Factories were springing up to feed the silk industry, which was now expanding with the new production methods, and flooding the world with cheaper and cheaper silk. They needed cheap labour.

Many families began to look to the new factories as a source of income, and Leung was no exception. All his six daughters would eventually wait every morning on the other side of the bridge for a ride to Guangzhou and a job in a silk factory, and my grandmother was just five years old when she joined her mother and older sisters on the factory floor.

When Lily talks about her time there her face clouds over and I can tell that her memories are not just vivid but still painful. The women and children worked 12-hour days, 7 days a week, among the deafening clatter of the machines, louder and stranger than anything Lily would have known in her childhood in the village. She was terrified.

The silk-worm cocoons were softened in vast vats of boiling water that steamed and churned constantly, then skimmed out and given to the youngest children whose small, nimble fingers were considered best suited to picking off the floss before the cocoons passed on to the next stage.

Tai Po and the other women spun the silk into thread on iron looms, and then the fibre was rolled on to drums. The factory was flooded with steam from the boiling vats which kept the air humid and ensured that the precious silk thread didn't break. There was little ventilation, and everyone struggled for breath. As the women leaned back and forth, back and forth across the loom, beads of sweat dripped from their foreheads on to the silk as it coiled into piles on the factory floor, a slow accumulation of profit for the factory bosses.

There were no such thing as workers' rights and the manufacturers wielded the power of any feudal landlord, exploiting the women and children as they fancied. For a short period, the shifts were even dragged out to 16 hours a day using the excuse that the Chinese must work harder than the Japanese in order to save China. The children's fingers peeled from constant contact with hot water and the fine thread sliced into the women's hands, but they had no choice except to continue to work.

When Guangzhou's swampy weather was at its most sweltering, the conditions indoors became even more excruciating. There was no let-up, and the children had to remain standing for the whole 12-hour shift. One day Lily couldn't take it any more and lost consciousness, slipping to the floor. She had barely opened her eyes again when the foreman seized her hand and plunged it into one of the open vats to 'wake her up' – anyone who held up productivity must be made an example of, after all.

Her hand began to swell and blister and the five year old burst into tears, in terrible pain. No other child or woman spoke up to defend her or take the foreman to task; not even her own mother, Tai Po, dared do anything. Young as she was, Lily understood that she must not protest, or else she and her mother and sisters would lose their jobs, and there were hundreds of other peasants who would willingly fill their places.

Later her mother comforted her, but she still cried herself to sleep. Her father had told her the story of the man who moved the two mountains, and Tai Po had explained that for a short period of sacrifice, a better life could be built in the future, and the little girl had to steel herself with those thoughts.

Meanwhile, Leung was determined to find a way to bring that better life to his family. Even though he worked in the fields like any of the other villagers, they had him marked out for his ambition. Leung had a plan, and now he set about putting it into action while everyone else carried on just as their parents had done before, whether out of fear of change or laziness.

I like to think that Leung's single-mindedness is a trait that runs down through the generations of our family all the way to his great-granddaughters. We have always been able to make the best of any situation. My grandmother was to transform herself from penniless immigrant to the owner of a flourishing business in 1950s' Britain, and my mother and father changed the course of the family's fortunes in the 1970s, but Leung was the first to lift us out of the cycle of rural deprivation.

He took the gamble of not selling his soy bean crop at the local markets, but turning it into soy sauce itself – a premium product that he could sell to the highest bidders as he chose. He set aside a small amount of farming land to build his tiny factory, a hut for processing the raw beans. He took on ten men to do the work, and as he had no money to pay wages, he promised them enough rice and soy to feed their families for half a year. They could barter the rice for other goods in the markets, too.

Like Leung, they were ordinary farmers with families, but now that the Guangzhou region was being sapped by share-cropping they had fallen on hard times and were grateful for the chance my great-grandfather offered. They were adaptable – they had to be – constructing the hut itself first, then becoming skilled and loyal factory hands.

Leung's plan of action was simple but effective. When the modest factory was built he split his team into two. Three or four were assigned to the harvesting and grinding of the soy beans, and the rest were tasked with carrying the endless buckets of water needed to dilute the pulp, or to lugging the tanks of finished sauce.

From the first day on, Leung would arrive at the factory to be met by a fresh crowd of desperate labourers begging for work. They offered to work for less than Leung's ten men, suggesting wages that could barely have kept them fed, but my great-grandfather remained loyal to his original workers and the agreement he'd made. He gave them a fair day's pay for a fair day's work and they gave their all in return. The soy sauce began to flow.

At this point, Leung contemplated his second gamble. He had to find a market for his product, and the restaurants and stalls of Guangzhou were the obvious place to start, but he decided to look further afield, with an eye to breaking new ground and driving up the business' potential, so he took a boat down the river to Hong Kong.

In the 1920s Hong Kong was booming. Life on the mainland had become increasingly precarious as rival political factions struggled to get the upper hand, and the ancient subsistence farming system clashed with a new industrial revolution, and the British colony had begun to look like a safe refuge – stable and prosperous. It had become cheaper and easier for immigrants to travel there, and the city's working-class population expanded exponentially. Guangzhou was already shipping most of its produce down the Pearl River into the maw of the British colony, and the openings for good products with enterprising salesmen were potentially limitless.

Sometimes they were fortunate and found work and a reasonable place to live, often they found less pay and even poorer living conditions than they had known in China. Seamen and labourers were worst affected, living cheek by jowl in buildings no better than flophouses, perhaps with ten or more strangers sharing a room.

Unscrupulous landlords rented the rooms by the hour, and some enterprising sailors sublet their bed when they were at sea, collecting precious whisky and cigarettes as rent. Every day they survived on a single portion of rice cooked as *congee*, a tasteless porridge that served as breakfast, lunch and dinner – a never-ending starchy monotony.

This was the Hong Kong that Leung was getting to know as he journeyed down river from Guangzhou to investigate, and it was part and parcel of the glamorous, decadent British colony. For years wages had remained stagnant as prices rose, and as Leung went from street to street he caught the mood of the workers. He witnessed firsthand the great seamen's strike of 1922, when Chinese protesters turned against the governor, demanding to be paid as well as non-Chinese workers.

He had never doubted his own peasant belief that men must continue to work regardless of hardship, but now he saw an entire city out on the streets in solidarity, from bus conductors to factory workers, clerks and sailors.

I would guess that the strike taught him two lessons – the power of the Chinese mob and exactly what could be achieved by sheer force of will; and that the Chinese, whether they have money in their pockets or not, love to eat. Throughout the strike the restaurants and eateries had remained buoyant, creaming a profit from the marchers. A reassuring thought to anyone in the catering business.

The restaurant trade was expanding rapidly and in every establishment from the high-class eateries to the lowliest street booths, every table bore a bottle of soy sauce, and every dish waited to be seasoned with Leung's own recipe.

Leung raved to Tai Po about the new life their family would have in Hong Kong, and his eyes lit up with ambition. All was going well, and if his hunch was right and he threw his back into hawking his soy sauce to every chef he could find, the potential was breathtaking. The family was on the road to prosperity.

chapter two

SOY SAUCE DELIGHT
HONG KONG 1925–1930

'A child's life is like a piece of paper on which every person leaves a mark'

每个孩子都是一张可画的白纸

When I was living in Hong Kong in 2002 and working as a lawyer, I found the city as exciting as it was overwhelming, a real assault on my senses. For my first few weeks there I was joined by Lily, my mother and father, brother and sisters, and we explored the city together. It was furiously busy, teeming with people going about their business at a frenetic pace against a backdrop of both the beautiful old colonial buildings and the modern high-rises, jam-packed with life. Pause for a moment on a street corner to try and take in the sights and smells, and you'd cause a pile up; the flow of humanity was unstoppable.

My mother had always been keen that I visit the place where she grew up; it held a special place in her heart. She somehow hadn't realised that it would be different though, and when she came to visit me there she was taken aback by the way the city had evolved.

The first thing she said – astonishing herself – was, 'I feel more British than Chinese.'

It's hard to imagine how much Hong Kong has changed since my grandmother first laid eyes on the city that rose above Victoria Harbour in 1925. She was a wide-eyed seven year old perched on her father's knee as they bobbed into the choppy harbour waters on the little Guangzhou ferry. Leung was moving his family to the city.

It's one of the deepest maritime ports in the world and the British had long been using it as a safe haven for boats of all sizes from the fierce and unpredictable storms of the Pacific. Ferries criss-crossing the port or ploughing the length of the Pearl wove their way around flotillas of commercial junks and sleek pleasure yachts. Beyond them Lily could make out a towering grey battleship at anchor, like a sleeping whale.

Their little boat hugged the coastline for safety, wending its way through scattered groups of small ragtag fishing boats swathed in loose rigging and weighed down by nets, barrels and crates. The crews lounged on the decks in the morning sunshine, and as the ferry passed they would rouse themselves and shout greetings, holding up their wares for the ferry passengers to consider.

Leung had made the trip many times, and knew how to turn them down with a friendly, confident wave of his hand. Lily looked past them to the city behind the docks, cradled in the lap of high green mountains. For the girl from a tiny village with just a handful of one-room shacks, the notion that every one of the spreading alleyways and streets was lined with huge buildings that were filled in turn with hundreds of people was unbelievable. She couldn't begin to take it all in.

The city was eating its way up into the lush, green forest that surrounded the harbour, and here and there she could see a new, winding road that disappeared up, up into the mist at the top of the mountains, as though the new urban sprawl led all the way to heaven itself. She saw the houses hazardously placed on the cliff edges, and worried that they might be blown loose and crash into the harbour below.

In the village the air had been dusty and dry, but as they reached Hong Kong the atmosphere thickened to something heavy and tropical, laced with the salty tang of the ocean. Over the splutter of the ferry's engine and the sound of seagulls and distant foghorns behind her, Lily began to make out the hubbub of the port itself.

Men shouted orders at running dockworkers, and chains clanked and ropes creaked around crates and barrels of cargo. The cranes trundled monotonously, hauling the goods ashore, and there were people everywhere, hurtling back and forth, shouting, smoking, jostling, joking. The scene made her heart race.

They put in at a high, concrete wharf which they scaled with a wooden ladder, before setting foot for the first time in their new home. The family huddled in a circle around their meagre pile of possessions as Leung paid the ferryman, and stared at their surroundings in amazement. Here the bustle of the streets spilled on to the quays, and there were sailors of all nationalities arguing with the Chinese dockmen in languages Lily had never known existed.

She had to look twice and stare hard at her first Englishman, who seemed like a giant. Twice as tall as her father, he had full round eyes and a thick blond moustache, his white linen suit as crisp as if it were made of paper. 'My mouth fell open!' she told me years later, and she kept on gawping as he strode right past her, away from the quay and out of sight among the rickshaws and motor cars.

Lily clung to her father's coat as she took in the scene; there was more noise and more to try to follow than she had ever known, even in the silk factory in Guangzhou. She was hungry too, after all the fresh sea air; they hadn't eaten since they left home and her taste-buds were pricked by the smell of fresh fish on ice and *char siu* pork slowly roasting on a dozen or more small fires. Fishermen, porters and sailors gobbled hot snacks in the little eateries that interspersed the shops, and Lily looked on enviously.

Seventy-seven years later, when I stood where my seven-year-old grandmother had stood before me on the now pristine Wan Chai harbour, I had to conjure up the images in my mind's eye. Land that would have been water in Lily's day had been reclaimed for the International Convention Centre, a huge modern building with a curving roof like a turtle's shell and glass walls. I didn't know which was more unreal, the Convention Centre or the knowledge that Lily had been here, and that the scene had been so different then.

Just then a lone street-trader appeared and wheeled a trolley laden with smoked and barbecued chicken skewers past the plate glass façade, and the smell went straight to my belly. Suddenly I was every bit as hungry as she must have been as she stood on the quay in 1925. Some things never change.

Hungry or not, Lily didn't have a chance to stand and watch the comings and goings on the quayside any more, as her mother Tai Po fussed and organised the girls so that they held hands in a chain, and Leung set off through the strange, narrow streets to their new home in the heart of Wan Chai, the densely populated hub of Hong Kong, on the north of the main island.

Leung was used to the sights and sounds of the city and led the way confidently, with his wife and daughters crowding close behind for safety, clustering out of the way of the passing bicycles or hand-carts which fought for position with the rickshaws. There were motor cars too, something my grandmother had never seen till that day, and then more scary still, the thin green trams that trundled by, the wheels giving off startling, tinny shrieks on the tracks. They jumped as the conductor clanged the bell and scattered the pedestrians who'd strayed into its path.

In my grandmother's village people barely walked with a purpose, let alone ran – nothing that urgent happened, but here the people of Hong Kong seemed to be moving at double speed. They made a blur of movement before the endlessly repeating backdrop of shop after shop draped with strings of lights, and long thin ribbons of signs which gave the businesses' names in columns of Chinese characters.

There were shops fronted by towering piles of cloth and racks of clothing in every colour, shops with glittering displays of trinkets, shops with giant cooking pans and woks stacked into columns, and shops with crates of vegetables that Lily couldn't even recognise, buttressed with sacks of rice and dry goods.

Red and gold lanterns swung overhead and hawkers kept up a

volley of special offers to pull punters out of the stream of potential customers passing by. Buyers and stallholders haggled loudly, passing a wooden abacus back and forth between each other, flicking the beads this way and that: first the customer would set his price, then the stallholder would seize the abacus and push more beads back, upping the sum. After a ferocious exchange, the deal would suddenly be mutually agreed, and all settled amicably.

Lily's mind was racing, confused by the barrage of new things to see, and the smells and tastes, and the constant buzz of the people around her; why weren't they overwhelmed too? What were they doing? Why were they rushing? They were Chinese like her, but their attitude and the way they gestured were different. They didn't dress the same either, and their accents sounded foreign to her as she heard snatches of conversation.

Clinging to her sister's hand she trailed after her family as they waded across wide roads clogged with people and carts, and shuffled through alleys where dozens of washing lines criss-crossed the narrow strip of sky above, as though spun by a giant spider. The voices of traders echoed down the alleys and the tiny squares, creating crazy, disorientating echoes.

They had barely gone a quarter of a mile when my grandmother was distracted by a cage of parrots that a vendor had wheeled to the roadside, and transfixed, let her hand slip free from her sister's. She marvelled at the green and gold plumage of the birds, a crystal clear image among the blur of impressions. She turned back, but the others had vanished.

She was surrounded by an impenetrable forest of legs, unable to see above the flow of people, and she spun on the spot, lost, with the metallic taste of adrenalin flooding her mouth. She was all alone, and began to be pushed and forced by the momentum of the crowd. Hot tears welled up in her eyes and she whispered for her mother, then yelled out loud. No one responded.

Suddenly she felt the heavy, familiar weight of her father's hand on her shoulder and the sound of his laughter as he hauled his weeping daughter up off the street and on to his shoulders, high above the crowd.

'Come on sack of rice. No time for crying. Keep up!'

Wan Chai literally means 'cove' in Chinese, and the settlement was originally a fishing village, but as one of the first areas of the city to be developed it was now crowded with ramshackle wooden buildings built in the typical Chinese bungalow style, then barnacled with extra rooms and extensions constructed from driftwood and corrugated iron. Over them rose the stately white colonial piles that dominated the main island: imposing symbols of British power and civilisation, some two or three stories high and lined with long, cool verandas. The slums of Wan Chai were huge, but still familiar to a peasant child, but the wider boulevards and squares gave the city the feel of a great citadel, keeping order over the chaotic alleys and shanty towns.

Leung had arranged for his wife and daughters to move into the home of his cousin and his own family, who worked as chefs. The place was no palace, and though the size and scale of Hong Kong dazzled my Lily, she remembered that their new quarters afforded even less privacy and space than the home they had left behind in the village.

Both families shared a squat, one-roomed erection with a flat tin roof, divided into two by a makeshift wall. There was one window, and Leung's cousins lived on that side of the hut, while Tai Po and the girls made do with the dark, airless back half of the building, where there was no room for furniture or any bits and bobs they might have brought with them. As they possessed only the barest necessities, this wasn't a problem.

At night both families slept head to toe on the floor, an arrangement complicated by the fact that it was not good feng shui to lie with one's feet pointing towards a door – that was thought to mean that the sleeper would end up in an early grave. Instead bedtimes were like a giant puzzle game as everyone tried to align themselves correctly while fitting all their limbs into the small space – more often than not someone ended up lying part in and part out of the doorway.

My grandmother's sleep was made nightmarish by a new horror: mice. Once she woke with a start to find one of the rodents gnawing on her hair. After that she slept on top of the wooden box where the family stored their bed linen.

Like many other villagers who were newly arrived in the great Chinese cities of that time, Lily's family kept up the old rituals that they'd brought from home, and following these rites helped to replace their culture shock with a sense of stability. Tai Po was a devout Buddhist and a believer in fortune-tellers, and as well as feng shui, she immersed her family in other ancient practices like acupuncture and ancestor worship, which is called *by sun* in Cantonese.

She observed traditional festival days and made use of Oriental medicine rather than turning to new Western drugs, and most of all she kept her peace of mind by performing t'ai chi, a form of exercise based around breathing and meditation.

It had been developed by monks over eight centuries previously and was known as 'meditation in motion' or 'meditative kung fu' to practitioners, who saw it as a kind of internalised martial art. At 5 a.m. every morning Tai Po would wake all the women of the family and together they would stumble to a nearby park to join other women practising t'ai chi in the early morning sunshine.

Women of all shapes, sizes and ages took part, beginning the swooping movements as if in a trance, swinging their arms smoothly into the postures and twisting their torsos as they placed their feet carefully and slowly lunged into each of the 'forms'. As she too followed the sequences, Lily was always amazed at the beauty and grace of the movements as the whole group shifted as one, even though there was no leader to direct them.

When I was new to London in 1999 and looking for new ways to make friends, I stumbled on t'ai chi. My mother had encouraged me to take it up because she thought it was a good way for me to exercise without injuring myself doing a 'real sport' and it was a very trendy thing to do in London at the time – well, trendy for all nationalities other than the Chinese, who associated it with their grandmothers, rather like bridge.

I found a class in an old church hall in North London near my flat, and started learning with a hippy crowd, made up of musicians with baggy, multi-coloured trousers and pony-tails, and vegetarians who preached world peace and nut cutlets. When they found out that I loved my steaks and worked as a commercial lawyer it went down like a lead balloon.

As if that wasn't annoying enough, the first question most of them asked was, 'Where are you from?' to which I'd reply, 'Manchester', and they'd look disappointed and try again, 'I mean, where are your *parents* from?' When I finally gave in and said, 'Hong Kong and China' they would smile with satisfaction. It all made sense now. 'Ah, you're Chinese.'

Being the only Chinese person in the class gave me some street cred at least, and some of them even assumed that I was there to support the teacher, or that I was a visiting t'ai chi master from Hong Kong. As we closed our eyes, breathed in unison and moved from pose to pose, I was actually meditating on one of the New Zealand students who I'd got a bit of a crush on. I hoped t'ai chi might being us closer together.

After a couple of months of lessons I learned that he had a girlfriend who happened to be a model and was so distraught that I gave up t'ai chi altogether. It may have been beneficial to my body, but the classes didn't do much for my self-esteem after all!

My great-grandmother took it far more seriously; she needed t'ai chi for the relaxation and mental focus it provided, and the early morning meditation helped her empty her mind of the day-to-day worries about money, and Leung's business, and the clashes with his cousin's family in the one-room shack. She prescribed it for her daughters so that they would grow up strong and elegant, and believed that it would fortify their immune systems and keep them healthy in the slums of Wan Chai. She even claimed that regular practice could improve their characters, giving them will-power, grace and good humour.

Lily wasn't an attentive student, and she wasn't helped by her sisters who took it in turns to try and poke her with their feet and make her laugh when she was trying to concentrate. It has to be said that while Tai Po and the other women relished the meditative aspect of t'ai chi, they also used the morning sessions for swapping gossip and scandal, and I think that must have been every bit as therapeutic as the 'flows of energy' they got from the martial art.

Returning to the shack, Tai Po began preparing the first meal of the day in a cramped kitchenette that only had room for one person at a time. It had two small stoves and a tiny, rusty sink. Makeshift cupboards hung precariously on the peeling walls, and if you accidentally knocked against them – a common enough occurrence in the kitchenette – chunks of dirt would crumble into the food below.

When she first arrived she wanted to get into the cupboards to reorganise whatever was inside them and scrape a little more space, but the cabinet doors were greasy and black with filth, and when she listened, incredulously, she could hear a mouse squeak somewhere inside. She never opened the cabinets again.

Tai Po had gone from being the mistress of her own home to being totally reliant on Leung's relatives for both money and shelter; she was little more than an unwelcome guest trying to keep her crowd of six little girls under control. She found herself being treated as an unpaid servant, taking on the lion's share of the housework. It was difficult for her to find paid work with her heavy, peasant accent and she stayed at home and kept the youngest girls by her side, realising that it was too dangerous for them to play outside. The friendly communal square in the middle of the village had no equivalent here in the city. She was desperately lonely, and beginning to feel like a prisoner.

In the end she found her freedom and independence in food – how typical of my family! She volunteered to do the grocery shopping for the entire household, and staked out a few hours of liberty a day, where she made all the decisions, picking out the best vegetables or pieces of meat she could afford, arguing with the stallholders and holding her own as she could not do back at the flat. These times quickly became sacred to her.

Then as now, the fruit and vegetable stores in Hong Kong were a spectacle in themselves. There were eight different types of greens bundled and stacked into separate mounds to choose from, and Tai Po would cast an expert eye over them, picking out only the tightest buds of *bok choy*, with its white stalks and dark green leaves, or *choy sum*, a premium *bok choy* with a more delicate flavour.

There was *gai lan*, which is still a family favourite – sheaves of blue-green leaves ten to fourteen inches long hiding miniature, broccoli-like florets and sold in 2lb bunches. In pride of place among the leafy greens were the *gwa* or 'fuzzy melons', mild squashes which were covered with a fur of prickly little hairs, and dangling at the end of the display were beans a foot long, with a crisp bite. They were cheaper than the other vegetables and essential for filling out a soup or stew.

The same scene greeted me in Hong Kong in 2002, and I used

to cut through the street markets on my way home from work just to feast my eyes on the mountains of *bok choy* and *gai lan* in alternating greens and inhale their fresh, crisp scent. As I walked down the narrow gangways between the stalls, the market workers would call out to me, 'Hey pretty lady, great discounts for you!' and I'd turn and smile, enjoying the compliment. I realised that they said the same to everyone, but it was a harmless, pleasant kind of attention, and I wondered whether my great-grandmother too had enjoyed the banter on the streets.

Tai Po and I were both strangers in the city, but the mere sight of all those goods laid out for our delectation was a tonic and a shot to cure homesickness, because everywhere were reminders of village food or the dishes my mother prepared back in Manchester for my sisters and I when we came home from school.

I recognised the dried, fermented black beans which gave meat, seafood and poultry a salty and pungent seasoning, and 'cloud ear' fungus, paper-thin, crinkly inch-long leaves stacked high. Lily's kitchen shelves had jars of 'cloud ears' sealed and hoarded for as long as possible, to be used sparingly in an occasional casserole – a real treat.

Then there were the stalls which specialised in mixing *heung fan* or 'five spice powder', ground from Chinese cinnamon, cloves, fennel, Sichuan peppercorns and star anise. Tai Po, Lily, Mabel and I all grew up with its familiar mixture of aniseed and the dark sweetness of the cloves, and I bought it to marinade spare ribs just as Mabel had shown me in the kitchen of our family takeaway. In Hong Kong the spice was displayed in huge open baskets in unimaginable quantities, and I worried that a gust of wind would create a storm of spice and send me into a sneezing fit.

It's been said that the Chinese will eat anything that walks on four legs with its back to the sky, and Leung joked with Lily that only the tables and chairs were safe from their voracious appetite. In Hong Kong food and business were what drove and animated the city, and the two thrived hand in hand, a rich, constant current that gave everyday life both its flavour and its character.

New restaurants opened daily, often one next door to another, and each hung up a long, thin cloth sign proclaiming its name, until the streets were fluttering with this colourful bunting, all clamouring for the passer-by's attention. In 2002 the descendants of those traditional cloth signs were winking neon strips in strident pinks, greens, blues…dazzling and disorientating.

Leung's timing was good, because Hong Kong had just been introduced to a new culinary innovation: *dai pai dongs*. These were little more than small metal trolleys operated by street-hawkers and serving quick, filling snacks: highly flavoured preserved bean curd and *won ton* noodles, Shanghai dumplings stuffed with meat and vegetables, wet soup dumplings and rice parcels.

The cost of setting up in business with a *dai pai dong* was low and the competition fierce, so for the first time good food was affordable for the masses in the city. The food was hot and fresh and cheap; snacking was rapidly adopted as a Chinese institution. If you had the appetite, and couldn't resist the delicious scent of the steam rising from the trolleys on the street, you could eat from morning to night.

As Leung well knew, every cook and every customer seasoned his food – whatever dish it might be – with soy sauce, and he had only to get a foothold in the trade to be guaranteed a steady income. He had plenty of competitors too, but his timing gave him another advantage: patriotic feelings were running high.

Both the Chinese and the Japanese claim the credit for soy sauce, and both use it heavily in their cuisine. The Japanese say it was invented by the Buddhist monk Kakushin, but the Chinese believe his recipe was already well-established in their own country, and all he did was to popularise it in Japan. My grandmother can only remember Chinese soy sauce, because the Japanese versions were boycotted in Hong Kong.

Leung's sauce was 100 per cent Chinese from its recipe to its ingredients to its salesman. The soy beans were taken straight from the field to be steamed and softened, and then mixed with special seeds and roasted, crushed wheat which balanced the soy flavour with a malty sweetness. This mixture was left to sit for three days until it settled into a dry mash called *see yow peen*, which was blended with salt and water to form *see yow gorn*.

The paste fermented in huge tanks until the flavour had deepened to its fullest, and was then poured on to great cloths which were folded and pressed, straining out the raw soy sauce. This was then refined and pasteurised before being poured into barrels, ready for consumption. These barrels Leung sold directly to restaurateurs and retailers who purchased both light and dark soy sauce – the light variety was saltier and used for flavour, the dark for colour.

In Hong Kong Leung made a basic wooden cart which he could load with several heavy barrels of soy and then he set out on foot to find his customers. My grandmother Lily went with him, exhilarated to be out of their dingy living quarters and exploring the city. She had never seen a restaurant before she came to Hong Kong, and to her they were fascinating and theatrical.

As Leung poured samples and cut a deal with the owners, Lily sat outside on the cart staring in, catching a whiff of the elaborate dishes ordered by the diners as the waiters shot out of the kitchen with steaming plates of food, set them down briskly and collected the little silver plates full of cash for payment. Everything was a drama.

Rumours were started and spread, illicit lovers met and there were impossibly elegant women dressed in embroidered silk *cheung sams* who seemed like otherworldly creatures compared to her own careworn mother. They dined with revolting fat businessmen whose faces, steamed by the soups and hot rice before them, perspired with heat and greed.

The waiters often adored her, slipping her morsels of food or doughy buns, and laughing at her precocity. One gave her a tiny tea cup set with matching chopsticks that fitted her small hands to scale, and she would copy her father, swilling a drop of soy sauce round the cup to test its flavour. She didn't care about staying at home with her mother and sisters – why should she when there was so much to see and so many exciting things to do?

Her natural strength of character was bolstered by the long hours on the street with her father, and she began to grow more and more determined and ambitious with her independence. Leung, with no son to lavish his attention on, encouraged his little girl and she watched him closely, learning all the while.

One important lesson that she picked up was the idea that learning English could give a Chinese person an entrée into that other, parallel world that ran side by side but separate from the slums of Wan Chai and the *dai pai dongs* and the bustling harbour: the colonial community of Hong Kong. She needed to master the language if she was to raise herself out of Wan Chai, and there was one place which offered Chinese of her class the chance to take lessons: the Union Church on Kennedy Road.

When she had finished her chores and been excused by her parents, Lily would faithfully make her way up the mountainside towards Victoria Peak and the church, and knuckle down to try to grasp the strange new language. The priest insisted that only those who converted to Catholicism could join in, in the hope of keeping out freeloaders, and Lily pragmatically went through the motions and renounced Buddhism. This, she felt, was a small sacrifice to make for her chance of an education, although she was only paying lip service to her new 'faith'. In her heart and at home she continued to be a Buddhist.

The walk to the church was an education in itself. Victoria Peak is the highest point on Hong Kong Island, and its extraordinary views and the cool breezes it enjoyed meant that it was staked out by Westerners and transformed into a suburb of grand, elaborate houses and high privilege. The only Chinese who passed through the area were servants and maids.

It was quite a spectacle for a village child. Sometimes Lily even took her sisters with her to see the palatial houses set on the cliff edge with their steep, sweeping driveways and tall iron gates – homes fit for princesses, with manicured lawns and busy casts of Chinese staff.

Here Lily could observe at close quarters the ethereal Western women with their pale skin and peculiar hair – not black and straight like her own, but lighter, and sometimes even curly. They wore fine silks and cottons in styles that bore no resemblance to anything she had seen a Chinese woman wear, not even the glamorous *cheung sam* ladies in the restaurants. But what Lily still remembers is the way that she was transfixed by the colour of their eyes: clear blues and sharp greens. She thought they were exotic beyond belief.

Years later, Lily, my mother and I retraced her daily journey and trudged in the sweltering heat along Robinson Road, which runs horizontally beneath the peak across the Mid-Levels and connects Magazine Gap Road in the east with Babington Road in the West. It's still fairly grand, though now it's been swallowed by the city, and there are soaring blocks of serviced flats looming over the old colonial properties that are set far back behind thick stone walls.

As we made our way along the road, Lily suddenly stopped outside one of the houses and announced that we were there, 'but everything has changed', she added, her voice falling. A worried looking white face appeared at a window, surveyed us as we stood on the pavement outside, then vanished. My grandmother rallied, 'You see, foreigners have lived in Hong Kong for decades, but they do not understand us Chinese. I worked here as an amah for years but we lived in separate worlds.'

'You worked here?' I asked.

'Yes, as an amah, it was my ticket to England.'

'Amah' is a job description that covers an array of domestic duties – an all-purpose housekeeper, a maid, a nanny. We had always known that my grandmother had worked in Hong Kong, but we had assumed she was a cook rather than a maid, so this was news.

One day when the young Lily was peering as closely as she dared over the fence at one of the forbidden palaces of Robinson Road, she noticed a young Chinese girl not much older than herself standing outside one of the residences. She was dressed in a plain black silk dress and standing by a large iron pram, holding an English baby who was crying loudly.

The baby was extremely fat, and its chubby tear-stained cheeks were resting comfortably against the girl's shoulder. She was bouncing it gently and cooing to it, desperately trying to settle the child. My grandmother had seen her sisters do such a thing many, many times before, but the sight of a Chinese girl with a Western child so startled her that before she could collect her thoughts she cried out in greeting.

The girl, also somewhat taken aback, replied. My grandmother went up to her and introduced herself, and took a closer look at the baby. Its skin was fair and smooth, with a pink flush to each cheek. Lily took the baby's tiny hand in her fingers and said hello in her best English accent, and magically the baby stopped crying and broke into a huge smile. Lily was enchanted.

The other girl grinned too, in sheer gratitude, and told Lily that her name was Eva, and that she worked as a junior amah for the judge who lived in the house. Shyly, they talked a little as Eva settled the baby in the pram, until an older woman wearing a black dress to match Eva's marched out of the house and up to the gates and opened them. She shot Eva and Lily a foul look, and ordered Eva back into the house. As the woman closed the gates, Lily waved at Eva, who snuck a surreptitious wave back.

Intrigued, Lily made a point of returning to Robinson Road at the same time the following day, guessing that the baby had a regular time for walks in his pram. She was right, and she didn't have long to wait before Eva appeared again. She was making her way up the hill, pushing her valuable charge in the immense pram. She recognised Lily at once and the two girls fell into conversation.

They had a lot in common as Eva's family also lived in Wan Chai, and she walked up the hill every day to begin work on Robinson Road. My grandmother added another ritual to her busy life, meeting Eva every afternoon outside the gates of the big house, and walking with the young amah and the baby in his pram round the streets and the public gardens of Victoria Peak.

Eva became my grandmother's best friend and her inspiration; Lily was only eight, but she had a new ambition – to live on Robinson Road like Eva and look after a Western baby. Still too young for the job, she quizzed Eva and redoubled her efforts at learning English to bring her dream closer. On Robinson Road in 2002, my grandmother pointed out the house of the judge that Eva had worked for, and though, despite her best efforts, my grandmother had long since lost touch with her old friend, I could tell she remembered her keenly.

I worked intensely in Hong Kong too, taking in long hours and full weekends in the office. I couldn't even take the time off to see my family to the airport when they left. It gave me fresh respect for the Chinese culture of hard work, and I realised that to these people, business will always come first. Being there helped me to understand what kind of energy it had taken for my great-grandfather to lift himself and his family out of the village near Guangzhou and slog round the streets of Hong Kong in the 1920s.

The soy sauce business was slow to start. Leung left before dawn and returned to his wife and children only after the last restaurant was shut. Several times a month he would return to the village to oversee the production of the sauce and keep an eye out for any light-fingered insiders who might be helping themselves to the goods.

In time the first regular contracts with the restaurants came, but it had cost him much to get that far, and on top of the expected running costs he had to bribe the local authorities to ensure that the soy sauce got a safe passage down the Pearl to the colony. There was barely enough left over to sustain the family, and precious little time for him to spend with them.

However, his work began to pay off, and his clients mushroomed – from restaurants and street stalls to retailers, they were all demanding customers with a thirst for soy sauce. The money started to come in, and eventually the family were able to see the benefits of their new prosperity.

The left the shack and took a modest flat of their own in Wan Chai, overlooking the harbour, and Tai Po could preside over her own household once more. The sheer space was luxurious to Leung's six daughters who had known only cramped one-room huts all their life. There were new clothes too, and for the first time since they left the village, regular meals.

I'm prepared to bet money that there was something generous and sumptuous about those meals too, because everyone in my family loves to eat. They must have seemed like feasts to Lily and her sisters. As they sat back in their chairs, satiated at last, Leung would make a great show of teaching his girls how to sample soy sauce like a professional.

First, he would pour a small amount into a glass and swizzle it around before smelling its bouquet with great ceremony. Then, with the sombre authority of a university professor he would talk about the sweetness of its aroma as the sauce settled into an inky puddle at the bottom of the glass. The true test however, he warned, was in the taste, and he would dip a bamboo chopstick into the soy and place a drop on the tongue of each of the girls. Finally, with much show he would sample a drop himself, smacking his lips loudly before declaring that the sauce was, of course, perfect and delicious.

It was a family joke, but it was also a celebration of everything that the aromatic liquid had brought them. As the family tucked into fragrant jasmine rice sprinkled with Leung's soy sauce, they would take turns to tell each other what had happened to them that day, competing to tell the funniest stories. Lily had plenty of material in her tales of the opulent life of Robinson Road.

Life was good at last, and as the months passed Hong Kong no longer seemed so alien as the island revealed its mysteries to them. When they were out by the quayside they often saw families who had just arrived from the mainland – their eyes wide, startled by the noise and bustle, faces dirty and clothes tatty, they clutched a small pack of their possessions to themselves in fear. Lily confessed to me that she would always point at them and laugh her sophisticated city dweller's laugh, quite at her ease.

'Now, now, Lily,' her father would reprimand her, 'Don't you remember your tears when you got lost looking at the parrots? Not so long ago, that was us.' The days of work in the fields and the pig rodeo and the horrors of the silk factory seemed like another life-time to the young girl, but like it or not, the family was still tied to the village and Guangzhou, and news of their good fortune was reaching the ears of enemies they did not even realise they had earned.

chapter Three

BITTER MELON

GUANGZHOU, CHINA 1930

'If you are patient in one moment of anger, you will escape a
hundred years of sorrow'

忍一时风平浪静 退一步海阔天空

I never knew my great-grandfather, and nor did my mother. Lily never really mentioned him to her or to me, until one day when we were browsing round the aisles of the Chinese supermarket together and she picked a bottle of soy sauce off the shelf and said, 'If only my father had known. There is nothing which will affect someone so much and so little as his own death,' and with that she turned on her heel and marched off round a corner into the next aisle. Her dark words left me stunned. Our weekly shopping trips were usually a time for gossiping and giggling, not weird prophetic statements.

Not wanting to miss this rare chance to learn something about my great-grandfather, I grabbed the bottle of soy sauce from the shelf and pursued her, hoping it would jog her memory again. When I caught up with her and asked her what she'd meant, my grandmother waved her hand dismissively – a characteristic gesture she used to shrug off any questions she didn't fancy answering. 'Just the ramblings of an old woman,' she said, avoiding my eyes. I persisted, and sighing, she said cryptically, 'All you need to know, is that soy sauce can be mixed with virtue but also with vice.'

Now I was starting to fear that my grandmother might have finally gone senile. A soy sauce bottle is found in every Chinese kitchen and on every Chinese dining-table. If my grandmother had developed an irrational fear of soy sauce, she had chosen the wrong culture to do it in. I pressed her a little more, and she looked at me squarely, 'If it wasn't for soy sauce, I might have had a father to look up to, and my mother, a husband to love her. And you,' continued my grandmother, 'might have had a great-grand-father to guide you and love you as I do.' Seeing she was upset, I apologised for pushing her to tell me so much.

'I know, you want to find out more,' she said, 'but it's not the sauce, it's what it symbolises to me. Soy sauce reminds me of the fine line between ambition and greed in men. My father was a good man, an ambitious man, but those around him were full of greed. When greed motivates men, they will do anything. Take anything. It consumes them and then they consume others. When such men set eyes on my father ...' she paused. Even 80 years later, her words were heavy with pain. 'They took our home, our busi-ness ... They took everything.' And then she told me about Leung and the journey to Hong Kong, and what happened next to the family as the business started to take off.

Back in the village where Leung's sauce was produced, little had changed while the family were away in Hong Kong. Their former neighbours were still trapped on the land, and the summer of 1930 was not kind to them. Poor weather led to a poor harvest, and the results were disastrous for the villagers – there was barely enough food to keep them fed, even when they ate only one meal a day, and there was no surplus to sell. For a community that already lived a hand-to-mouth existence, starvation was inevitable, and the weakest suffered most.

Despair hung over the huts around the lake. Those who worked for Leung were fortunate: the only chance most families had was to find non-existent paid work or to sell something, anything. Men were prepared to go to great lengths for food or money. Many were already making plans to follow Leung's example and travel to Hong Kong to find labouring work, knowing that even the lowest paid job in the city was worth more than many families' annual livelihoods put together. Chinese families are close-knit, but it was worth having an absentee husband or father in order to see food on the table.

When I interviewed Chinese immigrants for positions at Sweet Mandarin in 2004 I discovered that little had changed – the same situation continued to play itself out. Money made in Chinese restaurants in far-off Britain was sent home to feed the relatives and children left behind and great sacrifices were made for the sake of family.

Leung was still travelling back to the mainland to supervise the manufacturing end of his soy sauce business and check that there was no problem in transporting the barrels down the river. After five years of persistence he had had the pleasure of seeing his business grow exponentially, and was beginning to move serious bulk: the days of trudging the streets with the little wooden cart were long gone, and he sold direct to distributors across the colony. Leung's sauce sold as fast as he could make it, and still his customers wanted more.

The same villagers who had once toiled alongside him in the fields now saw him coming back from Hong Kong as a 'rich', changed man. His manner and his clothing were more confident and refined, his complexion smoother – he ate regularly now, and wasn't exposed to the harsh sun and numbing winters that the peasants had to weather. People took note.

Even more men flocked to his factory every morning as soon as the doors were opened to beg for work, but for every job that came up there were at least 15 bankrupt farmers fighting to be taken on. Leung was a good man who felt a responsibility to his kin and his fellow villagers, and he would have employed them all if he could, but his wealth was only relative and he could only take on as many as it was possible for him to pay. Leung had become that most cruel of things, a victim of his own success, and a target for grievances.

He'd set up his business in competition with several established soy sauce producers and merchants in the Guangzhou region, most of whom came from middle-class families and had inherited their companies from their fathers. They had done little to expand them, and were happy to be complacent. Others were not much more than one-man bands who recruited cousins and brothers to help out when demand picked up, then let them go when sales slackened off.

They were small town businesses with small town attitudes, focusing only on Guangzhou and the region round it where it was easiest to make money. They lacked Leung's vision and it had never entered their head that cheap soy sauce manufactured in their home province could be sold for such a sweet profit in Hong Kong, just a short river boat ride away.

They didn't like to see this peasant newcomer doing so well for himself, and they were watching him closely as, one by one, their businesses were eclipsed by his – not that they were shamed by his greater success, they were infuriated, and they wanted a piece of the pie.

It was around this time that Lily remembers her father returning to their flat in Wan Chai from a routine trip to the village in a wild rage. Weary from long hours of work and the ferry trip down the river, he snapped at the children and scolded them for playing noisily. Tai Po remonstrated with him, but my grandmother could see that his eyes were alive with anger.

Over supper the truth came out. Leung had been approached by a rival soy sauce maker who had demanded that he sell his business to him at a ridiculously low price. This man, Mr Wong, had made it clear that Leung had no choice in the matter, and no chance of negotiating a better price: there would be serious consequences if he refused. Leung didn't hesitate – he told Mr Wong to get out of his sight, yelling that no one would threaten him that way. He had built the business by himself, and he would never hand it over for a pittance. Mr Wong drew himself up and left in silence, leaving Leung spluttering with rage on the factory floor, barely able to believe that the man had had the nerve to threaten him.

Mr Wong was true to his word though, and Leung's point blank refusal did indeed have terrible consequences. It was not simply a matter of two fellow businessmen arguing, because to his rivals Leung was an upstart, a low-class opportunist who didn't know his rightful place – breaking his back in a paddy-field and being grateful to his 'betters'. He had added insult to injury and caused Mr Wong to 'lose face'.

There are many profound cultural differences between East and West, but the complex hierarchy created by the concept of 'face' is one of the most difficult to understand. For the Chinese, 'face' defines the self-image and the credibility of the person with whom you are dealing. It's also a way of showing deference to those higher up the social ladder – people who set themselves above you by virtue of their wealth and birthright.

In ancient times, Chinese warrior chiefs would commit suicide if they were defeated in battle, rather than accept loss of 'face'. In modern Chinese business, a subordinate never criticises their boss in public. My own parents taught us never to insult or embarrass anyone, yell or cause a fuss, because they believed that the shame we might bring to the family would be unforgivable.

Leung's rivals were not used to rejection, and they were determined to teach him a lesson. My great-grandfather didn't have to wait long: a few nights after Mr Wong's visit the thatched roof of his factory caught fire. Later my great-grandfather discovered that there had been witnesses who had seen the first flickerings of flame, but didn't raise the alarm because they knew about the disagreement between Leung and Mr Wong – word had spread quickly round the countryside, and everyone had been waiting for something to happen. They were cowed by the dispute between the 'big men', and kept their heads down.

These men just watched as the fire consumed the tinder-dry roof and began to eat into the walls, then to ignite a store-room of soya beans and wheat and send a cloud of thick smoke drifting across the village, making the livestock panic and sending roosting birds shooting up into the sky in search of fresh air. Leung's men were alerted and raced to the hut to put out the flames, reaching it in time to save the bulk of the structure.

By the time news had reached Leung and he had hurried up the river to see what damage had been done, the sun was up. The roof of the hut was blackened and smouldering, and here and there splinters of timber were still glowing as they lay where they had fallen on the factory floor. A large area of the thatch had burned right through, leaving the equipment and sacks of beans open to the heavens, and vats of soy sauce heavier than a man had had to be hauled away to prevent them being spoiled. Among the debris were Leung's men, sooty and exhausted but doggedly fighting to clear the mess and get the factory back into production.

When they had done the best they could, and a makeshift

cover had been crafted across the hole in the ceiling, Leung called time, left his weary workers huddled in the factory drinking cold lemon tea and stepped out into the daylight to try and think straight. He felt anxious.

He had no intention of caving in and selling his business, not when he had invested so much of himself and his family's hopes in it, but the audacity of the attack made him fear what might be to come. His mind a jumble of different thoughts, he reflected that he was grateful that his family were safe in Hong Kong and wondered what he would face next – how he could deal with Mr Wong?

He had trouble at home too; the business was demanding more and more of his time and now he was going back and forth from Hong Kong to Guangzhou every other day, striking endless meetings with restaurant owners and suppliers, then snatching hours to do all the paperwork on his own. Like many small businessmen he found it impossible to let anything in the company happen without his watchful eye overseeing it. He would have done everything himself, if he could.

His little girls were oblivious to the extent of his fears, only thinking that Mr Wong had been dismissed and that things would go on as before, with Leung's business growing from strength to strength, and more treats and feasts to come, but Tai Po was growing weary of never seeing her husband. She was beginning to lose patience.

My grandmother's last memory of her father came from the day of her twelfth birthday. Leung made time for the party and the family came together, swapping stories once again, on a day that was benign and sunny. Lily was especially happy – her birthday present was a new jacket, and she wore it all day, proudly modelling it for her sisters to admire. Friends started to arrive just before lunch, and after the meal they were planning to visit another family's home.

Leung was in good spirits, as though he had decided to forget his troubles for a day. He carried Lily on his shoulders, sang her songs and told her stories he'd heard in restaurants. When she recalled this, she told me how proud she'd been to see him and know that he was her father. By now she knew from what she saw in her friends' homes that most Chinese men showed little or no interest in their daughters, and that Leung was different, and his daughters knew they were loved and wanted.

They celebrated as my family always celebrates, with food – lots of food. There were plates of roasted meats, heaps of white rice, dishes piled with fresh vegetables crisply fried in a wok and, as a centrepiece, a huge fish soused with soy sauce and ginger which made my grandmother laugh because of it's bulging, startled eyes staring up from the platter. Even today she loves fish head because she says its flesh has the smoothest texture, especially the eyeballs.

Before they tucked in, each member of the family took a stick of incense by turn, lit it and placed it in a plant pot. The little ritual celebrated both Lily's birthday and commemorated the family's ancestors, because the incense was meant as a miniature representation of the huge, bell-shaped coils of incense that burnt all day long at the temple. It was a cleansing rite, and the fragrant scent fended off evil spirits and attracted good.

This low-key, domestic approximation of a greater and more solemn ritual was an integral part of daily life in Chinese society. You burned the incense to keep the family safe from generation to generation, and it became a torch linking past, present and future members of the clan. Hong Kong means 'fragrant harbour', after the glades of incense trees that flourished in the land around the port, and the Chinese incense that was shipped all round the world from the city.

As each sister, then Tai Po and Leung added a new stick to the pot, the room filled with heady fumes and my grandmother found her eyes watering. She was welling up with tears of joy as she sat there in her new coat, surrounded by her family and friends before this lavish feast. The party began in earnest and everyone attacked the spread of dishes, talking eagerly and laughing loudly, the happy buzz ringing round the walls of their modest dining-room. The sound of celebration drifted out of the open windows and beyond the balcony, out into the afternoon sunshine.

Lily was in heaven, but no sooner had the last dish been scraped clean and the last set of chopsticks laid down, than Leung announced that he needed to make a trip up river to the factory because a new consignment of raw materials had been delivered and he wanted to check through them. Tai Po's face fell, and she asked her husband why he couldn't take a single day off work to celebrate their daughter's birthday.

Leung wearily rolled out the argument he used every time: 'If I don't work, who is going to feed you all and buy your children new clothes?' and Tai Po knew it was impossible to fight with him. The family had never dreamed they could live so well, and they owed everything to Leung's dedication. There before them on the table lay the remains of the lavish birthday dinner – the fish's bones picked clean, the last few grains of rice in the bowls – a reminder of how far they had come. She had to let him go.

Leung was weary of it too, and when he'd fetched his coat he gave Lily a final birthday hug and bid his family goodnight, his heart heavy. As he walked down to the harbour to catch the ferry, he consoled himself with thoughts of the future – the business had survived the fire, and as the orders rolled in he could think not only of repairing the damage, but improving the factory too, and stepping up production.

Maybe he went on walking, pacing the deck of the little ferry to Guangzhou on the warm late-summer evening, watching the calm, deep blue South China Sea roll by as the boat cut a swathe through the waves. On the ferry he couldn't do any work. He had to give in and relax, the only lull in his frenetic day.

The next stage of the journey to the village brought him back down to earth, as he jounced and rocked in a small cart over twisting dirt roads that he'd come to know so well that he'd memorised every pothole. He was still thrown from one side of his bench to another by the sharp turns, and by the time night had fallen and they had reached the bridge that led into the village he was grateful to climb down and walk.

The factory was still, apart from the night-watchman whom Leung dismissed. He closed the heavy wooden front door behind him and lit an oil lamp. Piles of paper were strewn across his desk waiting for his attention, and a smaller pile of urgent contracts. His managers had been thorough, but Leung needed to check everything they had approved – on a few occasions the wrong sums had been invoiced, losing him money. He didn't know for certain if the mistakes were accidental or deliberate but he had a workforce and a family who relied on him to keep the business tight, so he couldn't afford to let anything slip. Knowing he had a long night ahead of him, he shook off his coat and settled down to his ledgers.

At this point the story becomes unclear. Leung was disturbed by an intruder – perhaps someone who had been hiding somewhere in the building for hours, maybe behind one of the vats or in the store-room; perhaps someone who let themselves in after Leung when he left the door unlocked; perhaps even someone that Leung himself had let in. The police reports called this mysterious man a 'thief' but he took nothing.

There was a struggle – the papers on the desk were disturbed and there were signs of disarray on the factory floor – and then the man had grabbed one of the metal crowbars that lay handy for plying open the crates and swung it without mercy at Leung's head. The bar connected with Leung's brow with a dull thump. He was probably dead before he hit the floor, and that's where he was found the next morning, his blood puddled with soy sauce that had leaked from the nearby barrels. Next to him lay the crowbar, where the thief had dropped it before he raced out into the night, leaving the factory door wide open in his panic.

My great-grandfather was murdered in the village where he was born. His workers were greeted by the sight of his twisted corpse in the dark pool of blood when they stepped gingerly round the open door in the early hours of the morning, and they turned tail and fled, scared that they would be implicated. A few hours later one of the foremen arrived and had the courage to call the police.

Of course it could not be proved that the mysterious 'thief' had been sent by any of the rival merchants, and the police in rural China had nothing by way of forensic equipment so no one would be able to trace the stranger. Leung's run of success had ended in a flash of cold metal in the night, and he had paid for his ambition with his life – dead at 37, leaving a wife and six daughters.

The village was in a state of shock. Back in Wan Chai, Tai Po had woken and begun preparing breakfast for the girls before they got up, yet there was no sign of her husband. It wasn't unusual for him to work so late that he even slept at the factory, but he was always back in Hong Kong before dawn to see his clients.

There was a knock at the door, and she opened it to see Leung's nephew, who was struggling to keep his composure; he bowed his head and, as calmly as he could, told Tai Po what had happened to her husband. It struck her like a physical blow, knocking the breath from her body and making her head spin. It was too much to take in and she struggled to focus on Leung's nephew as his quiet words rang in her ears, louder even than the early morning street sounds of Hong Kong, then she cried out and doubled up in pain.

Lily and her sisters were woken by the noise and stumbled out of bed to see what was happening. Leung's nephew had managed to draw Tai Po into the apartment and close the door to the street, and now the six sisters crowded in the living-room doorway to hear the terrible news.

Lily was inconsolable, howling and screaming that she wanted to join her father in the grave. She was no more than 12 years old. At that age, I had my comfortable home and had just started secondary school – my biggest dilemma was choosing whether to be a violinist or a lawyer – I am her granddaughter, but I can make no comparison between our lives at that point. I never knew what it was like to lose an adored father and to see my future snap shut before my eyes.

That day changed Tai Po for ever. As a child, my own mother lived with my great-grandmother years after the murder, and young though she was, she could sense that something had broken in Tai Po. Panic and grief filled the space in her heart that she had kept for Leung; she could only tell my mother again and again that she was lucky to have a future to look forward to. Tai Po had never been alone, going straight from her parents' house to Leung's, and now she had no companion, the family had no breadwinner, and there was no son to provide for them in his father's place.

In the flat in Wan Chai the weeping went on for days, the family barely able to eat or sleep. Tai Po moved through the rooms like a ghost, empty and alone; she could barely contemplate living, but left the children in the care of a friend and returned to China to set about arranging Leung's funeral. She remained there for some time.

She needed an explanation, something to lessen the shock and give her a chance to do something for her husband, but the crime was not going to be solved. She racked her brains, and as she always did at times of trouble, she turned to the Chinese traditions that had seen her through their move to Hong Kong and the early days with Leung's family in the Wan Chai slums.

Tai Po lay awake, lost in the thought that their ancestors had punished the family for not burning enough paper ingots to honour them when the business was booming. She set up a small red and gold shrine for Leung outside the village and placed his photograph at the centre, then burned paper notes for him and prayed fervently that he would protect his family in death and rest peacefully in the afterlife.

She took up her position there and mourned her husband, alternating tears with prayers. As custom dictated, she poured wine three times on the spot on the factory floor where he had died, anxious that he would not become a restless ghost and haunt the building.

The villagers watched her grief, and discussed the family's fate. It was common knowledge that they had bad feng shui – first the three sons had died, and now Leung. Tai Po agonised about the factory and its feng shui – she had always known that it was wrong, and now she began to blame herself for not insisting that Leung reorganise it so that its energies would be balanced. Feng shui or 'wind and water' lies somewhere between a science and an art-form, a belief that through the proper balance of human existence with the natural order, life can be harmonious and generate good *chi* or spiritual energy. Something in Leung's family was out of kilter, condemning them to tragedy.

Tai Po spent precious money on a feng shui master whom she hoped would be able to save her own and her daughters' future, and he divined the exact location for Leung's grave. It lies in the hills behind the village, close to his factory, and Tai Po marked it with a small stone with a tribute carved in red: 'Loving husband who gave everything for us.'

On the day of his burial she could barely stand, and had to be supported by other mourners, her pitiful cries echoing across the hillside. Leung was lowered into the earth, and the ceremony was performed solemnly. Dressed in black robes, with her face gaunt and white with misery, my great-grandmother returned to Hong Kong, but she left her heart and soul in the village where she and Leung had been married.

The city to which she returned was irrevocably transformed. Hong Kong had symbolised an escape from the drudgery of farming, a magical, sometimes frightening place that had offered and delivered opportunities that were the family's salvation; it had been their ticket out of poverty, and their home. Without Leung, Tai Po was stranded and bankrupt in that same city, unable to imagine how she could feed her daughters or control what would become of them.

Their fall from grace was brutal. Chinese law dictated that

Leung's soy sauce business – still thriving, despite losing its driving force – could not be passed to Tai Po but had to be handed over to her husband's next male descendent instead. Women could not own property, so Leung's nephew inherited it all, and Tai Po and the six girls could only turn to him and trust him to be benevolent. He was under no legal or even moral obligation to provide for them under Chinese tradition.

They presented themselves to him, hoping for clemency, but he didn't have Leung's fair-mindedness. Casting an eye over the six sisters, he announced that he would only take in Tai Po and the girls if one of them agreed to be his cousin's concubine – they were now his property to dispose of as he chose. The girls knew the cousin in question, a bitter man, and Lily remembers his smile, which was slow and menacing, and unnerved them all – she tells me he had a vicious temper which they'd witnessed many times.

The idea of living with him as man and wife was repulsive to the sisters, and Tai Po steeled herself for her daughters' sake and proudly refused, standing by their wishes. Slighted, the relation cut Tai Po and the girls off without a penny, the earth barely settled on Leung's grave.

There was no social security system in China, no poorhouse or church-run charities to help the destitute. The family had no savings. Unable to afford their rent they returned to the back room of the shack in Wan Chai, to the only support they had – Leung's uncle and aunt. In the few years that they had been away, even more migrants had swelled the population of the slum, and the conditions were medieval. The homeless squatted on rooftops or lay comatose in the streets. Its inhabitants' prospects were bleak, as confined as the narrow alleys and subdivided rooming houses – Leung's girls had come full circle.

His relatives may have meant well when they took in Tai Po and the girls, and it must have been clear to them that Leung's widow was breaking down – but their hospitality soon soured. They thought that Tai Po had developed airs and graces to match her husband's spectacular business success, and they took it upon themselves to teach her a few lessons about the reality of their lives in Wan Chai.

Tai Po and the girls were servants once again, and totally dependent on their new 'masters'. This time Tai Po did not have the energy to assert herself or find a means of escape. She was immersed in sadness, and lost interest in defending her daughters. There was nothing she could have done, in any case, without jeopardising what food and shelter they had.

Lily suffered most of all. Hong Kong had been her playground, and now it was cold and indifferent. There were no more trips to marvel at the restaurants, and she was no longer the pet of the waiters and the soy sauce buyers. At the heart of it all was the gnawing, numbing knowledge that she would never again have the father who had been her greatest ally and who loved her so much, the man who told her that if she was determined, she could change the world.

She tortured herself with the idea that she was responsible for her father's death – after all, he had died on her birthday. With a child's logic she turned her enthusiasm for that lovely feast and all her gifts into an outrageous demand for her father to earn more and more money to indulge her. Deep down she was convinced, childishly again, that if only she had been with him when he made that final trip, she could have saved his life – raised the alarm, perhaps, run for help or struck out at his attacker.

She was realising that no one cared if her family lived or died, and her great-uncle and aunt took great pleasure in teasing and bullying her. They gave her errands to do, threatening that if she didn't jump to it and do it just as they said, she'd be out on the streets. Like a dog, they made her wait while they ate, then gave her only the scraps from their table. Their jealousy of Leung was sated as they laid into his bereaved family, taunting them with their helplessness. Watching her mother sink into a deeper depression, Lily bit her tongue and began to think of ways to try to save her.

My apartment in Hong Kong was in Wan Chai, and it had long since been gentrified, barely recognisable as the old quarter of the city where my grandmother mourned Leung. When she visited, I took her out for a walk in the area to see what she would make of it, and in Southern Playground, among the picnickers and the basketball players, she stopped and smiled to herself.

In her time, the playground was used as a labour market where workers called 'coolies' waited for work by the hour or by the day. In the evening it was transformed into an open-air working-class 'nightclub' where men who had been lucky enough to come by some cash could meet to spend it on food from *dai pai dongs* or watch performers demonstrate kung fu and magic tricks. There were prostitutes working the crowd too, young women little older than Lily's elder sisters.

Lily and her sisters did not go there at night, but they did make their way there early every morning to find what work they could after Leung's death. Mostly the jobs were small and paid little more than a tip: carrying groceries, delivering parcels or letters, collecting dirty laundry. They sewed table-cloths for restaurants, too, keeping their heads down and their minds focused on earning money for Tai Po, who left them largely to fend for themselves in her depression. They couldn't afford to mourn their new life but they could still work, and that would save them.

My grandmother swore to herself that she would take work anywhere but in a silk factory. She wanted to prove herself and win her independence again, and free her family from Leung's relatives. They didn't need luxury, only to determine the course of their own lives once more. So she worked and considered her future, biding her time.

Six long months passed, and the time came for Tai Po to fulfil her final obligation to her husband. The Quingming festival is celebrated every springtime in China, usually in April, and a literal translation of the name is 'clear brightness'. It marks the time when people welcome the new season and honour the rebirth of nature after a harsh winter.

It's also traditional for people to use it to sweep and tidy their loved ones' graves and remember the dead with a ceremony rooted in Chinese ancestor worship called *hang san* or 'walking the mountain'. Families gather to pay their respects with tributes and gifts at the graveside. When I was little we kept up the custom, heading to the cemetery armed with incense, paper money, paper models of cars and houses, and a sumptuous roast piglet dripping with oil and honey. The paper effigies were offered to appease my hungry ancestors and give them currency in the afterlife, and as we burned them they gave off a flame that lit up the Chinese characters on the tomb.

At Quingming that year, Lily and her family pooled what little money they had and made their way back to the village for the first time since Leung's death and burial. She told me that she was genuinely afraid, thinking that they had been so altered by their father's death that the villagers would treat them with contempt, just like Leung's relatives in Hong Kong.

To her surprise, the families in the hamlet greeted them with open, sympathetic arms, finding oranges and sweets for the girls. They remembered Leung as a benevolent employer who had supported many of the families in the village with a steady wage when the crops were poor, or when there was no other work to be had in Guangzhou.

Lily was not just back among friends, but cradled in memories of the past, better times, when her father was still alive. They remained in the village for a few weeks but in the end Lily knew with a sinking heart that she could not stay even if she wanted to. She had become a city girl. She was also scared that her father's killer was still out there somewhere and she worried that he might come back for the rest of them too. Once more she was lost. She didn't feel safe in Hong Kong under her great-uncle's thumb, and now in the village she was being cut adrift from her past, from her father and now her own failing mother. She did not belong anywhere any more.

The morning of the family's departure came quickly, and while her sisters methodically repacked their bundles of goods, Lily slipped away to the hills were her father's grave lay. As she walked up to the site she picked wild flowers from the roadside, tugging a thread from her jacket – the one she'd been given for her birthday, a lifetime ago – and used it to tie them into a bunch.

She knelt at the small shrine her mother had built and gently laid the flowers before her father's photograph in its small tin frame. Tears sprang to her eyes. Looking at the picture, she saw herself reflected in the glass side by side with her father and realised for the first time how alike they looked. The photograph was fading from exposure to the sun, and she felt as though Leung were slipping away into the spirit world before her very eyes; this was her last chance to be close to his spirit, and summoning all her strength she asked out loud for her father's forgiveness.

Now she swears to me that as she spoke, a gust of wind rose on the hillside, rustling the leaves on the trees around her, and she took this as a sign that Leung had answered her. She smiled at his image, and touched her fingertips to the glass. It was time to move on; he permitted it. She wiped her eyes on the back of her sleeve and stood up, suddenly hearing her sisters calling to her in the distance.

Turning her back on her father's grave she ran downhill to join her sisters and her mother as they walked to Guangzhou. Lily would not see the village again for 72 years.

chapter four

JADE AND EBONY
HONG KONG 1930s–1950s

'If you bow at all, bow low'

一不做 二不休

*O*ne Sunday during my family's visit to Hong Kong, I arranged to meet them outside the HSBC tower, a giant Norman Foster-designed skyscraper which stares out across Victoria Harbour. As they approached I could barely hear their cries of greeting because the air was filled with a loud, high-pitched clucking, like a flock of very talkative flamingos. It was an extraordinary sound like nothing I'd come across in Hong Kong.

Intrigued, we made our way towards the noise to see what on earth was making it, and found a café at the foot of the building filled with Filipino women chattering away over breakfast in their native tongue, and comparing the jewelry they had just bought. The architecture was amplifying their voices and making it sound as though there were even more of them.

'What are all those women doing there?' I asked my mother.

'I think they are the amahs,' said my mother.

'Amahs? Maids? All of them?'

'It's Sunday – they all get a day's holiday on Sundays. I suppose this is the only place where they can meet.'

Now, to understand the unique role of the amah in Hong Kong society, you must first understand class. Hong Kong's class system was one of Great Britain's less welcome gifts to the colony; while money had always separated the urban rich from their poor counterparts in China, the British added a layer of social convention to the divide, and gave it a clearer definition. It became as difficult to transcend as the class system back in the UK, and it was racially based: Westerners first, Chinese second.

Though foreigners had lived in Hong Kong for generations, few of them had any inkling of the day-to-day hardships faced by the Chinese who worked for them, and certainly no clue about the backwards rural life in the villages. There wasn't much crossover between the ex-pat world and tough life of the Chinese in the streets and slums.

Amahs bridged that gap. These trusted Chinese maids were usually the mothers of families of migrant peasants who spent their days, and most of their nights, serving as butler, babysitter, seamstress and cook to the wealthy families that employed them. They worked long hours without complaint, leaving their own children to be raised by their parents and pouring their wages into supporting three generations of their families.

Between the 1930s and the 1950s, amahs, always a colonial institution, rose in popularity. Chinese women began to supersede Chinese men as the household servant of choice – they would, after all, work for half the wage, HK$5 to HK$15 a month, versus the

HK$30 demanded by male servants. They were a financially shrewd option. They were also indispensable, doing all the tasks that were considered to be beneath uppercrust foreigners, and negotiating in baffling Chinese with tradesmen to make sure their bosses weren't short-changed.

In England I never knew a family with a maid – to me they only existed as characters in period dramas with white caps and aprons, but in Hong Kong they were still part of the fabric of life. As a young woman my grandmother had served in the grand homes in the city just as those Filipino women now did, and to her it was a fresh chance to make her way in the world. I wonder if she could have known where it would lead her.

When the ferry from Guangzhou arrived at the Wan Chai docks, my grandmother braced herself. The excitement of seeing old friends in the village and the high emotion of making her tribute to Leung had made her forget what her life was now like in Hong Kong. She moved like a zombie with her sisters and mother through the crowded streets on her way to her uncle's tiny shack, and as she climbed the front steps she was filled with a deep yearning to have her father there by her side, protecting her. The others dragged their feet too, unwilling to step back into their lives as skivvies.

To their surprise, their obvious grief seemed to have softened their aunt and uncle, who appeared to have had a change of heart. They met them not with their usual sarcasm but with sympathy, food and drink. As they settled Tai Po and the girls, and produced dishes of rice and soy sauce, Lily felt claustrophobic, not trusting their new friendliness. She wanted to leave immediately.

Her mother noticed her shifting uncomfortably and tried to pacify her. She called Lily over and demanded that she greet her aunt and uncle politely, but Lily couldn't hide her feelings. She didn't move, glaring at them instead, and the more her mother tried to coax her to sit and eat with them, the more difficult it became to swallow down the grief and loss that was rising up in her throat.

She wanted her father back; she wanted to be safe, and to be free. She leapt up and ran blindly out of the shack and into the streets, pushing people out of her way, her eyes filled with tears. She ran till her lungs ached, not caring where she ended up, and when she finally came to a breathless and exhausted halt she found herself once more standing on Robinson Road.

Eva was on the drive, and when she recognised her friend she ran to greet her, sweeping her up in a hug and chattering as though they'd never been apart. Lily told her what had happened and Eva heard her out, then reminded her friend about her dream of working as a junior amah. Lily was old enough to find a job with a Western family now.

She gave Lily the address of the agency that had found her the job in the judge's household and started to tell her what to expect when she went to see the owners, and how she should dress and answer their questions. Lily listened gravely, and as they walked up and down Robinson Road together planning what she should do, she felt as though she was slowly coming back to life for the first time since the news of her father's death – her future was opening up again.

I can imagine how the hills around Robinson Road brought a feeling of calm to my grandmother. You couldn't imagine that bad things could happen there – in Eva's tales the paintwork was never chipped or peeling, the curtains were always clean. The scent of floor-polish mingled with the perfume rising from the flowerbeds where there were always plants in bloom, replaced by diligent gardeners as soon as their petals dropped. Robinson Road had become a touchstone, its very existence promised something that she could aspire to, and the knowledge that a girl just like her, Eva, had escaped to its rarified world, redoubled her ambition.

The next day she went straight to the agency in the heart of Hong Kong Island. Its offices were based in a smart-looking building with a gleaming brass plaque at the door and a large, airy waiting-room. She told me that as she perched on the edge of one of the room's large, leather armchairs under the slowly spinning fan her feet barely reached the carpet. After a short wait, her name was called and she was shown into an imposing office.

The owner sat behind a large desk, a slight-looking Western man in a pin-striped suit. By his side stood his wife, every inch the severe and starchy Victorian matron, with her hair in a bun and an ankle-length hobble skirt from another era altogether. The owner wrapped a pair of wire-framed glasses round his face and consulted a large, leather-bound appointments book. Lily's luck was in – the agency was in need of new girls to take on junior amah positions.

Lily's heart soared, but the Victorian matron soon damped her spirits as, hands behind her back, she began a brief but intimidating description of the reputation that the agency enjoyed and their insistence that all girls followed what she called the three 'P's' – promptness, politeness and polish. In a clipped voice she laid down the rules.

There were no set holidays or rest days – they must be requested in advance. Employers usually allowed girls one half day of rest for religious observances, such as the first and fifteenth day of the month according to the lunar calendar. Thinking only of shiny marble hallways and gentle afternoons pushing the pram in the park with Eva, Lily signed all the documents before her and was hustled into the second office by the matron.

Now she learned the extent of her new duties. If she was one second late or did not fulfil her tasks to her employers' satisfaction, she would be fired on the spot. That would mean that she was blacklisted by every single agency on the island. No one would entertain the idea of employing her as an amah again.

She attended a series of hour-long lectures on the scrupulous housework required to reach Westerners' standards. She learned to make beds with sheets, check above cupboards for hidden dust and polish intricate pieces of silverware. When cleaning a room, the windows should be closed so that the dust would not fly around as the floor was first swept, then dusted, washed and finally polished. A good amah cleaned the house from top to bottom every day.

Then there was the laundry. Linen was scrubbed in soapy water and run through wooden roller mangles. Cold water starch was applied before ironing clothing, which must be made stiff to the touch. She had to master flat-irons and judge their temperature so that they were neither too hot nor too cool for the job in hand. The creases on trousers must be straight enough to stand comparison with a ruler. If the girls did not adhere to these standards they would be returning their tunics to the agency.

The instructions were endless, and knowing my grandmother she was probably tempted to daydream them away, but the agency provided set routines and mnemonics for everything from shining brass to ironing lacework. There was no way of skimping on this training, so Lily paid attention and by the time she had been in service for a few months she had the procedures down pat.

When her training was judged to be complete, Lily was issued with the traditional uniform of a junior amah, a white tunic over black trousers, the cost of which, she was told, would be deducted from her salary over the next six months. She was to report to her first assignment at 6 a.m. the following morning.

As she left the office with her uniform tucked under her arm in a brown paper parcel and a slip of paper with the address of her new employers, my grandmother literally jumped for joy. I know this, because I've seen her demonstrate that irrepressible little jump on many occasions – usually when she's had a modest win on the lottery – and when she's excited she hops up and down, and giggles like a schoolgirl. I wonder what passers-by in that rich part of town thought as they saw the young Chinese girl with the big, exuberant grin celebrating her new beginning?

Despite her time spent observing the natives on Robinson Road, my grandmother's entry into the world of foreigners in Hong Kong came as another culture shock. She had never actually been into the house where Eva worked, nor spoken to any foreigners other than the husband and wife who ran the agency. Now she felt that she was truly 'abroad'.

The very smell of the houses was strange, the feel of the clothes she had to wash was different and their food ... how could meals made with meat and vegetables bought on the same island taste so alien? The language was a mystery too, as although she had picked up a few rudimentary phrases of English during her lessons at the church, she couldn't hold a conversation, nor understand much of what was said.

In any case, in most houses there was a strict hierarchy among the servants themselves, and junior amahs did *not* join in with family activities. She was to be seen and heard as little as possible, a household help who remained in the background. The Westerners gave commands in pidgin English, though sometimes they communicated with Lily only by pointing, nodding and smiling. She would eventually pick up English by listening to the more senior servants talk with the families, and silently going over what they said in her mind later on.

Over time many senior amahs became confidants to their mistresses and surrogate mothers to their children. While the relationship between amah and boss was ultimately a financial one, it was not unusual for a genuine affection to develop between them. At the top of the servants' hierarchy were specialist cooks and 'baby amahs', and Eva and Lily eventually worked as a nursery nurse and a cook for wealthy households. For now she was an 'all-purpose servant' who cooked, cleaned and minded the children as demand dictated.

When I worked in Hong Kong my bosses at the law firm were mainly British men and women with public school accents. Far-sighted Chinese colleagues would argue that the company needed to let more senior Chinese lawyers rise through the ranks and become partners, but their arguments fell on deaf ears. Business in Hong Kong was still dominated by the culture of the 'expat'.

Even in 2002 the British seemed to retain their habits and eccentricities more rigidly than they ever had back home in the UK, and lived in a mini-England in the Peak area. In the 1930s there was an even higher percentage of British people running the great banks and the legal and political structure of the colony, and they were more British still.

They educated their children in separate schools and took jobs only in British-run firms and societies. They sat down to tea at 4 p.m., had a roast dinner after church on Sundays, and they organised tennis tournaments at a country club where the only Chinese were the staff. They insisted on Irish bed linen over Chinese, which they considered inferior. Their bathrooms were marble with silver taps, their suits were tailored to perfection and totally impractical for a monsoon climate, and they all spoke like the Queen. They ran the world.

Their superiority was manifest. They occupied the grandest, most expensive houses on an island where lack of space meant that there were hardly any houses at all. The threw parties that were enchanting and brilliant, showcasing their wives who dug out their finest jewelry and bathed for hours beforehand in tubs sprinkled with expensive imported bath salts. Nothing but the best would do.

Lily would watch enthralled as she held a tray of cocktails for the ladies who circulated in their slivers of evening gowns on the arms of gentlemen in immaculate white dinner suits. The British set the precedent of decadence, luxury and glamour which still personifies Hong Kong today.

The British men who were dispatched to the colony looked on their plum jobs as a birthright. They were frequently talented and ambitious, boasting connections to royalty or the highest echelons of the British government. They expected a good life too, and they found it there. Their families were imported to enjoy the posting as an extended holiday, and Hong Kong's Chinese side gave it a titillating and exotic flavour – where else but in Hong Kong could an Englishman see people eating snake, pig guts, duck feet, pigeon, and even cats and dogs?

On the whole the British were, despite their domination of the colony, good masters to their household servants, whatever they made of Hong Kong at large. On rare occasions Lily could even find herself eating alongside her masters, though the majority of her meals were taken in a separate, 'non-public' part of the house. Casual mistreatment of servants was rare, and foolish too because amah networks established rules and boundaries of employer-employee relations that were strictly observed. Any boss who verbally mistreated a maid could expect to have word of it spread around the colony fast, and that would jeopardise their ability to hire amahs in the future.

The pay was good too, even though the standards were exacting and the hours long. Perhaps one reason why the relationship remained so good was that all the British knew that Hong Kong was only a temporary addition to the Empire. When the 100-year contract was up, Hong Kong would be back in the hands of the Chinese; the British were guests at the behest of their hosts, and ultimately their days were numbered.

My grandmother made it clear that she was proud to be an amah in those days – the job was a cut above those available to unskilled women, and it had pleasing long-term prospects. She passed through some of the most influential and well-heeled houses in Hong Kong, and most crucially, she learned to cook. Not just Chinese food in all its forms, for many of her bosses were partial to the local cuisine, but also delicacies from all over the world, depending on the nationality of her employers.

She was provided with a proper stove fired with coal, and the demands made on her could be challenging – it wasn't unusual for her to be asked to prepare dinner for ten at two hours' notice. But Lily could simply summon her sisters and other friends who were working as amahs and they would set to and deliver the meal on time.

These were the years when she learned to make the delicious 'claypot chicken' twice baked with shitake mushrooms, and created a savoury sauce for serving the sweet *lap cheong* sausages of the village feast days – both of which would become her signature dishes in England. She was learning to love cooking, above all, and to have the courage to experiment with ingredients.

When they tasted the results of her first efforts, the families would reward her with more money for shopping so that she could take her pick of the finest and rarest ingredients on offer in Hong Kong. One employer had a penchant for a fine fillet of beef with fat potato chips and a blanket of Béarnaise sauce, and Lily learned to choose and prepare a cut of beef so tender that the flesh seemed to dissolve on the tongue.

She loved her new career, even the dreaded cleaning routine that had been drilled into her at the agency: she came to take pleasure in a job well done, remembering Leung's perfectionism. What she found difficult was striking personal relationships with the Westerners, whether the children or, in one case, the wife of her employer.

This woman was bored and isolated in her imposing home and she would sit down with her young amah in the early morning or in the afternoon, when the children were at school and complain to poor Lily at length about her husband's mistress. Lily didn't have much experience in this field, but did her best to reassure the woman and try to tell her she was lucky to have such wonderful children and a house of her own.

As she spent hours on her knees waxing the endless oak floors of the house, my grandmother could go into a daydream and imagine that she was the lady of the house, dressed in beautiful silk clothing and commanding her own maid. A cry from the couple's baby boy brought her back down to earth and she'd be up in a flash, pulling off her gloves and hurrying to his side.

Her experience sewing table-cloths for restaurants and patching her own family's clothes was useful for mending holes torn in school uniforms and darning cricket socks, and she was allowed leftover pieces of cloth to take back to her family. Usually there was a sewing-machine and she was encouraged to make clothes from scratch using paper patterns. She learned to knit, too, making socks, scarves and tiny outfits for the babies. It's hardly surprising that she rarely took a day off for herself.

Once she had overcome some of her misgivings about letting herself get fond of her bosses' children she found that she got great pleasure from her bond with them – to the very young, she wasn't a subordinate, just Lily. For years after she had left various positions the children would continue to visit her and bring her gifts of money or food. She thought of and talked of the children as though they were her own.

For a while she switched from placement to placement before being posted to a Dutch family, the Van Houtens, on a permanent basis. The head of the household was the grandson of Coenraad Johannes Van Houten, an industrialist who had made his fortune by inventing cocoa powder. In 1825 he had come up with a manually operated hydraulic press that squeezed cocoa butter from cocoa beans, leaving behind a cake that could be ground into cocoa powder.

Chocolate was everywhere in the Van Houten home, and my grandmother quickly developed a sweet tooth. She remembered one show-piece dinner party where every guest was given pieces of a jigsaw made of Van Houten chocolate and challenged to fit it together to reveal the family name.

Lily's main job was to look after the youngest son, a blue-eyed, blond-haired baby. Though the Van Houtens were a very pleasant family, they travelled extensively and were in and out of the house. They weren't particularly interested in getting to know Lily personally. She was even instructed to walk well behind the family when they were out in public and she was dandling the little boy.

Dinner was served at 6 p.m. precisely every day, the silver cutlery laid with precision on a spotless linen table-cloth. If Lily got a detail of the arrangement wrong, Mr Van Houten could fly into a rage. Not surprisingly, she never felt wholly at ease in his company. She tried to shrink into the background when he was present, but the only time she could truly relax was when the baby was asleep and she could slip off into the kitchen or the gardens.

In the end her peaceful life on the Peak was shattered not by Mr Van Houten's tantrums but something much greater, because not long after the little boy's first birthday the Japanese launched their attack on Pearl Harbour, and now the second Sino-Japanese war accelerated into one of the most ferocious theatres of battle in World War Two.

The Japanese Imperial Army moved swiftly to invade and occupy the British, and US colonies that now make up Malaysia and the Philippines, Singapore and of course, Hong Kong. The British forces were soon overwhelmed by the speed and ferocity of the Japanese attack and made a forced surrender on Christmas Day, 1941, to Isogai Rensuke, the first Japanese governor of Hong Kong. Both the Chinese and the British came to refer to that day as 'Black Christmas'.

To the occupying Japanese, Chinese lives were worthless. One of the first things the new administration did was to cut civilian rations to near starvation level in order to conserve food for their own soldiers. It became unlawful to own Hong Kong Dollars, which were replaced by the Japanese Military Yen, and hyper-inflation wrung the economic lifeblood out of the colony.

Their cruelty to the Chinese has become infamous, and much of it was public. Caught in the occupation, Lily witnessed prisoners being beaten, tortured and executed, punished without a fair trial for attempting to escape or on suspicion of espionage. She does not talk about these times readily.

People took to barricading themselves in their houses, only emerging for hurried trips to buy what food they could find. Tai Po, finally in her own apartment, rarely left it. When she did, it was to exchange Hong Kong dollars for handfuls of rice.

Lily's experience of the occupation seemed unreal as the Dutch were not immediately at war with the Japanese, so she floated between two worlds – the horrors of the streets of Wan Chai and the bubble of the Van Houten's household, where things went on much as before. The Dutch and Japanese had been trading since the seventeenth century, and the Van Houtens had a lucrative contract supplying chocolate rations to the Japanese army. They didn't break off business until Japan invaded the Dutch East Indies a year later.

Mrs Van Houten helped in the business as Mr Van Houten's secretary, and where they went the rest of the family followed. Lily was terrified when she realised that she would have to travel right into the enemies' heartland with them, but there wasn't enough time to engage a new amah and she was too attached to the little Van Houten boy. Tai Po begged her to leave the post and find some job, any job, rather than risk the voyages, but Lily had to stand firm.

Most of the Western families had been shipped into camps by the Japanese, so her chances of getting another post as an amah were non-existent. The families that remained cooperated by necessity with the invading army. She concentrated on the little boy to try and quell her own fears, telling herself that he would be upset if he lost his beloved amah and found himself in the care of a stranger. The Van Houtens arranged for her to have some basic lessons in Japanese so that she could carry out her job when they were installed in the country.

The Van Houtens sailed from Hong Kong to Tokyo and back three times altogether on military ships with my grandmother and her charge. Occasionally she will relate a story, or mention a horrific scene that she was caught up in, but the details remain sparse. Each voyage took three days in each direction, and my grandmother found herself functioning as a go-between negotiating her way among both the Van Houtens, the Japanese and the Chinese who were on board.

The Japanese militia on the ship paid her close attention when they realised that she could speak English and a little Dutch and Japanese, and press-ganged her into learning more so that she could translate for them. There were Chinese prisoners on the boat that the soldiers needed to interrogate.

A woman who was half-Japanese and half-Chinese was assigned as her teacher, and she taught Lily not just the language, but also the history and traditions of Japan. She had grown up in Japan and wanted to be a geisha, but had been considered unsuitable because of her 'tainted' Chinese blood. She drilled my grandmother in the language, letting it be known that any laziness or failure to grasp the new words she was being taught would result in corporal punishment meted out by the soldiers.

Lily snatched time when she could to work hard on her Japanese and, in doing so, saved her own life. That intensive training rendered her at least useful to the Japanese soldiers: they put her to work translating simple messages and later the forced confessions of prisoners. Their brutality to the Chinese on board ship matched their actions on a greater scale in Hong Kong, and Lily played a difficult double game of doing the Japanese' bidding while trying to influence them to treat their prisoners better – the guards trusted her as they came to know her, and she became confident enough to speak out.

One day deep into the voyage she came across some soldiers who were about to rape a Chinese woman and cried out in Japanese, 'Imagine if that was your sister or wife! Save your dignity. This is a war between men!' She was appalled that she'd taken such a risk, but as she stood her ground, shaking with fear, she saw the expression on the soldiers' faces change as her words sank in. They exchanged glances, then spoke rapidly among themselves for a few minutes, too fast for her to understand. Then they apologised to the Chinese woman as she cowered on the floor, clutching her torn clothes to herself, staring from them to my grandmother and back again. Lily translated the apology for her and went on her way, her nerves jangling.

In the years of the occupation, Lily was relatively safe when she was working for either the Japanese forces or the Van Houtens, but whenever she went out into the streets of Tokyo or Hong Kong to shop or to visit her mother in Wan Chai, she lost that magical status and became just another Chinese woman.

Once when she was hustling through the streets on the island, eyes down, she was called to a halt by a group of Japanese soldiers who held her at gunpoint. Fearing a beating, or worse, rape, she made her case in Japanese, 'I am a translator for your people and am useful only if I live. Please spare my life. I need to get back to work for your officials.'

The soldiers were so shocked at the stream of words coming from this small Chinese woman that they spared her. Others were not so lucky. She tells me about a friend of hers, an elderly seamstress who worked for another family on the Peak, and who committed the fatal error of failing to bow when she passed a Japanese sentry in the street. He screamed at her and began to lay into her with a cudgel, beating her wildly; she died of a heart attack during the assault.

By the end of the war in 1945 Hong Kong was a shadow of its pre-war self: the Japanese' indiscriminate atrocities had halved the population and the economy was shattered. More than 80,000 women had been raped.

My grandmother has nothing but contempt for the war crimes that were committed, and sees those years as a bad dream from which she finally awoke, shaken, and began to pick up the pieces of her life, along with her fellow survivors. She chooses to say very little about the period and about the trauma of her experiences in the occupation; she prefers to keep her pain private.

The reign of terror ended almost as quickly as it had begun, as the failing Japanese nation surrendered after the dropping of two atomic bombs at Hiroshima and Nagasaki that August. The British moved swiftly to regain control: Hong Kong's colonial secretary Franklin Gimson left his prison camp as soon as he heard news of the fall of Japan and declared himself acting governor of the territory. His provisional government welcomed a British naval fleet into Hong Kong harbour a few days later, and with it hopes for a full recovery and the return of the prosperity of the 1930s.

Hong Kong's recuperation would be slow. It drew strength from the rise of Communism on the mainland as immigrants flooded in and companies moved their headquarters to the colony from Shanghai, evading the hostile Chinese government. Businesses of all sizes drove the rebuilding of the economy as a fresh generation of entrepreneurial Chinese rushed to make up for lost years and lost profits. Their determination to succeed and live by their wits saw the revival of gold, diamond and other financial markets. Gradually the colony began to boom again.

For Lily the years after the war were thrilling as the mood of Hong Kong began to alter, and a new type of society began to evolve. Perhaps because the Chinese and the British had suffered side by side under the Japanese, they found that they could no longer maintain the colonial status quo so strictly, and now the old taboos weakened. The British were no longer invincible, and the Chinese felt able to ask for a greater cut of the territory. Chinese who were wealthy enough could now buy property in the expensive 'white' suburbs like Robinson Road.

It was a time of great personal change for Lily too, although she continued to live with her mother in Wan Chai – Tai Po had not fared well in the war, too scared to leave her meagre apartment, and she was reliant on her daughters for income. Lily was now in her late twenties, with years of work to her credit. When the Van Houten boy was old enough to be sent away to school, she moved jobs, and this time the agency dispatched her to an English family, the Woodmans.

My grandmother still speaks of the Woodmans with great affection. In her time with these gentle people she learned what it was like to be part of an English family, drinking tea at three and going for long walks after Sunday lunch. She took so well to the English way of life that the Woodmans' friends called her 'the English rose with a Chinese heart'.

They were new arrivals in Hong Kong and in a sweet twist of fate, they had taken a house on Robinson Road, the very place where eight-year-old Lily had dreamed of living. She was engaged as a nanny again, to two small children. There was none of the formality of the Van Houten home here, and Mr Woodman was a most benign head of the household, endearing himself to all his staff.

He was tall and balding with slightly sticky-out ears, and when he smiled he showed his gums and his eyes creased up and all but disappeared, as though he was a parody Chinese, so his nickname among the servants was 'the Chinese Englishman'. He was responsible for the reconstruction of Hong Kong's entire electricity supply and a very important man in industrial circles, but his new home was extraordinary and perplexing to him, and the first hot and humid summer left him exasperated by the demands of his new job.

Lily had just arrived in the household and she quickly became indispensable as a guide to the city and an unofficial confidant. She could solve every problem, whether explaining that he would have to work on Saturday mornings like everyone else in Hong Kong, or pointing out that his spectacles were sitting on top of his own head, exactly where he'd put them before he lost them.

Her spirit of fun re-emerged with the Woodmans, who didn't expect her to stand meekly to one side and disappear into the background; now she truly felt as though she had a second home. It was as a companion to Mr Woodman's mother that she really endeared herself to the family.

Mrs Woodman senior was a heavily built lady in her sixties with failing health, a good heart and a low boredom threshold. She enjoyed Lily's company tremendously, and was grateful to have her – she did not write her off as a mere servant, or someone who was only there because she was paid to be. Even though Lily was much younger, the connection between the two of them strengthened into a lifelong friendship, and the older lady became a huge influence on my grandmother's life.

When my grandmother tells me about her time in Hong Kong with Mrs Woodman senior she loves to describe the walks they would take by the sea and down to a quayside to watch the comings and goings. They found that despite the differences in their class, their birthplaces and their age, they had much in common. Lily always admired out loud the white flowers that floated out on the water where the Pearl joined the South China Sea, loving both their beauty and delicacy, and their strength on the current.

It was Mrs Woodman senior who told her that they were called lilies, and it was those magical water flowers that inspired my grandmother to adopt the English name, Lily, for the rest of her life. She aspired to be as fine as the water lilies while being hardy enough to survive her life in Hong Kong, for although everything at Robinson Road seemed like a fairy-tale, her circumstances in Wan Chai had changed little.

Mrs Woodman senior had little idea of this, but she liked to ask my grandmother questions about her home life and her own family as they rode through the crowded streets of the city in the comfort of a taxi. My grandmother would answer, but she didn't try to make much of the differences between the two worlds. Mrs Woodman's curiosity was piqued though, and eventually she insisted that Lily show her how the Chinese really lived – she asked to see her home.

Lily was reluctant, but the older lady insisted and one afternoon at the end of a shopping trip she directed the car back to her street, in the slums of Wan Chai. She and Mrs Woodman kept up a stream of chatter, but as soon as the cab pulled up in the dark, narrow street Lily fell silent and felt her cheeks glowing red with shame.

The presence of Mrs Woodman, and her world of light, bright rooms and polished parquet floors, threw the misery of the place where she and her family lived into sharp relief. The street was teeming with people spitting and smoking, the air above them filled with strings of washed and darned underwear flapping in the wind. The gutters were blocked with gravel and there were weeds sprouting from cracks in the concrete walls.

Piles of wood scraps and rusting metal obstructed the entrance, and she had to help Mrs Woodman pick her way over them and up the dank concrete steps leading into the gloomy hallway. Mrs Woodman commented that Lily's home seemed lost and forgotten, and that she could not understand how someone could really live in such conditions.

The interior of the little apartment was even worse. Rubbish lay heaped in one corner and filthy cloths partitioned the rooms. It was chill and depressing, and the fumes from the kerosene stove caused a fug that made the old lady choke as soon as she set foot over the threshold. There was no plumbing, or running water, and the gassy stink was undercut by the acrid smell of stale urine from the chamber-pot of every one of the hundreds of people who called the block their home.

Mrs Woodman said nothing now, her hand clutching a hand-kerchief to her mouth and nose, and her eyes beginning to stream with tears when she realised how her friend lived, and what she had asked her to show her. She did not sit down, but picked her way fitfully around the mess. At last, turning to my grandmother with a wretched expression, she asked in a dull voice, 'How can Hong Kong call itself a British colony when you live in… in this *medieval* place?' Neither she nor Lily had an answer.

Mrs Woodman's concern for her amah's well-being was excep-tional; she genuinely cared about the plight of the local Hong Kong Chinese. Hundreds of thousands of refugees were flooding into the tiny territory from the mainland in order to avoid Chairman Mao's dictatorship, and the British colonial government had long been overwhelmed.

The slums of Wan Chai, still the first port of call for new residents, were filled to bursting point and makeshift camps were mushrooming at the edges of the colony. Charities and relief organisations did what they could to help the new arrivals, but most of them were left to fend for themselves in appalling conditions. Expatriate families with a conscience found evidence of the horrors of the slums encroaching ever more on their own lives, and often they were no longer comfortable living side by side in such inequality.

The final straw for the Woodmans came in 1953 when tens of thousands of refugee huts in a slum area burned down in a freak fire. They were scratchy constructions of driftwood and old packing crates and burned rapidly, trapping the multitudes of men, women and children who were packed inside them. The Woodmans could see the flames from the veranda of their house on the Peak, and the cool breezes that night brought the stench of burning refuse and human flesh.

The newspapers reported the carnage in graphic detail the next morning, printing stories of people racing down the streets with their clothes on fire, screaming horribly, and the charred bodies of children found huddled in the wreckage. The black and white photographs of the devastation confirmed the family's worst imaginings.

They knew that there would be no miraculous changes in the way that Hong Kong's poor eked out their lives – it was only a matter of time before another fire, a collapsing building or an outbreak of a contagious disease swept through the slums. There would be no legislation and no funding that would change this. The Woodmans could not in good conscience remain in the colony.

As the Second World War had given way to the Cold War, people could not help but wonder how long the new communist behemoth of China would tolerate a British presence in one tiny corner of its empire, and the colony's foothold seemed precarious. When Mrs Woodman senior suggested that she would like to go home to die peacefully, the family's minds were all but made up. They had been homesick for some time too, despite all the excitements of the Far East.

They didn't forget Lily though. They came up with an offer that was to become the biggest twist in my family's tale – a chance for my grandmother to escape the uncertainties and the biting poverty of life in Hong Kong. She could, they said, come with them to England as Mrs Woodman's carer. They were anxious not to leave her behind in the slums, but give her a new chance in a richer country.

Mrs Woodman, Mrs Woodman senior and the children would travel back to England that year, returning to Hong Kong only for short periods to be with Mr Woodman. Lily would go back and forth with them, though most of her time would be spent in England. When his work in the colony was done, Mr Woodman would go back to England too and the house on Robinson Road would be closed up and sold.

They must have known that it was a heart-wrending decision for her to make, but they did not know quite how hard. In 1953 my grandmother had a husband, her mother and two children who depended on her, and it was their faces that she saw as she tossed and turned for many sleepless nights, agonising as she weighed up a future life in Hong Kong against another, unknown one in England.

chapter five

FIRECRACKER CHAN
HONG KONG 1930s–1950s

'If Heaven made him, Earth can find some use for him'

天生我才必有用

My grandfather was not mentioned when I was growing up. To my sisters and I he was little more than an old photograph that stood in a cabinet over the sideboard in Lily's dining-room. The picture was at the centre of a small shrine that she had created in his memory. Next to the photograph was a plate of half dried-up, wizened oranges which served as a food offering to his spirit, and a small plant pot. A number of burned incense sticks stood in the pot – the only indication that Lily still honoured her husband.

As we grew up and my grandmother got older, she began occasionally to drop little stories about our grandfather – just the odd line – into a conversation, here and there. She delivered these tidbits as though he were still alive and standing in the next room, rather than dead and in the grave for 20 years. We learned a little more every time, and as always, it was odd objects or unpredictable things that would jog her memories.

We have a cocktail bar in Sweet Mandarin with traditional Chinese spirits to go alongside the Smirnoff and the Jack Daniels bottles. There's a strong spirit called *moutai*, Three Snakes Liquor, plum wine, lychee wine and rice wine all racked up in colourful bottles with vivid, enticing labels.

They may look innocuous but the alcohol is 40 per cent proof – enough to take the top off your head. We serve a snake blood cocktail which is irresistible to young men who want to prove their mettle on a Friday night out. One afternoon I was drinking tea with Lily in the bar when I caught sight of one of the bottles out of the corner of my eye and asked her jokingly, 'Have you ever tried three snakes' liquor, Pop?'

'Yes, but it's too strong for me,' she replied in a matter-of-fact manner. 'It's also more a drink to help you out ... you know.' She stuck out her little finger, making it droop comically and sugges- tively, then made it rise slowly up. She looked me straight in the eye and let out a wicked chuckle, 'At home, men drank to improve their performance in the bedroom.'

By now I was pretty embarrassed, but I wasn't going to let her win.

'OK, then. What about that one?' I asked, pointing to a dark bottle that had a picture of bamboo leaves and a girl dressed in a *cheong sam* on it. Lily's expression hardened.

'You can keep that one,' she said. 'Men always blame the wine, or the woman but it's not that ... when men intoxicate themselves, they allow themselves to be tempted.'

I had no idea what she was talking about. Had I missed some-thing? I waited, as it seemed as though she had more to tell me.

'No matter how much I hated his mistress, I could not blame her ...' My grandmother looked at me with a new seriousness. She wobbled slightly on her bar stool, as she were about to faint.

'Pop, are you all right?' I asked. Her eyelids fluttered.

'Sorry Helen,' she said. After taking a deep breath, she seemed to regain her composure. then her mood passed in a wink and she smiled again. 'When you are my age, there are so many memories, and not all of them are pleasant.'

'I don't understand, Pop.'

'That bottle was the brand that your grandfather used to drink and it ended up killing him. If only it had killed him off sooner.'

She was talking about the man she was supposed to have loved and I was shocked, but she looked down at her shoes, ashamed of the secret that she had hugged to herself for decades, and only now said out loud for the first time.

I changed the conversation hurriedly, and soon she was back to her usual self, but when she got up to leave at the end of our cup of tea, she turned and pointed to the bottle and gave me a final warning, 'That stuff is poison. Not just of the body but of the man himself. With your grandfather, it turned a good man bad.'

All I knew about my grandfather was contained in this kind of brief, cryptic anecdote, handed out in small doses by Lily. I wanted to know more about this man, and I set myself to finding out the rest of this muddled tale of the hurt that one human being can do to another.

He was called Kwok Chan and he was born in 1914, four years before Lily. He died in England in 1961, a year after his arrival. He had followed my grandmother to England and is now buried in English soil; every year Lily visits his grave and places a wreath on the stone then plants one incense stick behind it, one before it and a third pointing east.

When I joined my mother and grandmother at his grave one year I was also given three sticks to place, and performed this simple ceremony of respect. My grandmother had had many harsh things to say about him, and he had clearly hurt her deeply, but it was also transparent that she still had some affection for the long dead man.

My mother did speak fondly of him, but she would also confess, when pressed, that she did not know him much at all. She simply gave him the respect that a father expects from his daughter in Chinese culture.

We girls never stopped being fascinated by this shadowy relative, and as children my grandmother had to give us strict instructions never to lay a finger on the small shrine in the dining-room. I must have been about nine years old when my curiosity got the better of me and one day when Lily had left the house for a few minutes to go to the corner shop I took the opportunity of inspecting my grandfather up close.

The raid was hazardous: I had to climb on a chair and reach up, wobbling precariously, to grasp the frame. It was dusty, and I didn't want to leave any fingerprints, so I wiped it with the hem of my blouse and then gazed on my grandfather for the first time.

It was a head-shot taken in black and white, a man with close cropped hair, high cheekbones and the kind of eyes that had a spark of life that lit up even a dulled old print like this. His lips were full and his look was slightly feminine, very striking. His eyes had a certain sadness too. He bore an uncanny resemblance to my mother.

He was youthful and at the peak of his powers, frozen here in the photographer's studio at the beginning of his love story with my grandmother. Their love was unusual for the time – a marriage not arranged by relatives or village elders, but by fate itself and the kind of coincidences that a city like Hong Kong conjures up. I suppose that my grandmother chose to remember him as he was then, and not as he became, corrupted by the darker side of the city.

When I was in Hong Kong in 2002 I discovered for myself that Kwok Chan, like Lily, began his life in the Guangzhou Province. In fact, he was born in a village only a few miles from my grandmother's. It was larger than my grandmother's hamlet, and more affluent, and Kwok Chan's family were a cut above the local peasantry because they ran a popular restaurant. The village was close to the sea, and had more of the atmosphere and bustle of a miniature port, with fishermen and traders passing through. It had also been infiltrated by Triad members.

The slow, monotonous rhythm of rural life still prevailed though, and nothing happened at Hong Kong's hectic pace. Customers could spend all day in the restaurant, marking the passage of time with endless cups of tea and the odd intermission for food.

If there was a drop of rain, all activity in the village ground to a halt and everyone headed to the restaurant for a bowl of soup. In any case, after work the men would meet there to chew the fat and stay long into the night. There was a peripatetic clientele as well who passed through on long journeys and made a pit-stop to eat, drink and catch up on what was going on.

The little restaurant was truly the heart of village life, and Chan's father, Chow, presided over it like a benevolent monarch, a huge, smiling bear of a man with an impressive gut that was testimony to a lifetime spent in the food business. The locals knew him affectionately as 'Fat Chow', and as well as his reputation as a supreme host and *bon viveur*, he had the job of village storyteller.

Obviously there was no television in rural China in that period, but there were no travelling performers either, or rudimentary cinemas. As a storyteller Fat Chow re-spun folk-tales, lampooned characters in the village and even acted out dramatic predictions of a customer's future that he divined from his tea-leaves.

To the Chinese, being a storyteller is not about being original or plucking tales from thin air. They believe their golden age to be long past, so a good storyteller will transmit messages of good fortune and bad omens from ancestors. When he swirled tea-leaves or shook the incense sticks, Fat Chow was blessing the souls of his customers' ancestors.

A villager might arrive in a state of high anxiety and beg Fat Chow for a good word from the past, and when the amiable host could conjure reassurance from a cup of *oolong* tea the villager would go away relieved and thankful. A social service, you might say.

Fat Chow took his vocation very seriously indeed, gathering a wealth of ancient wisdom and sifting for the things that older villagers had known, but which had now become neglected or misunderstood. When business was slow, he would sit in the corner and observe his clientele, storing away impressions and anecdotes for future routines. His painstaking fidelity to this tradition and his ability to sink cup after cup of tea made him a master of his art.

His son, Kwok Chan, didn't seem to have much inclination to take up his father's role, or even the family business. He had his eyes and his ambitions fixed on the bigger world outside the village, to his parents' dismay. They needed him to help them, and he worked waiting on tables, preparing food and spending long hours dozing in the corner, bored out of his mind, while his father chatted to the regulars.

He felt chained to the family and the restaurant, and by the time he was a teenager he found work in the restaurant torturous. He wanted to see some more of the world, or just to experience something new after years with Fat Chow's tea-leaves and the slow plod of the village routine. Naturally he gravitated towards the less desirable customers who passed through the restaurant, and he found a way of marking out his own niche. He took up chess.

Chess was popular, but chess was also a gambling game – this being China, after all. Most evenings, a few pairs of players would take up their regular perches on two bamboo stools set up on either side of a rickety bamboo table. The chessboard was drawn on a sheet of thin paper and the pieces were hand-carved from scraps of wood. Bets were laid down.

Most of the players were casual gamblers spicing up the evening's game, but some were professional hustlers who could make a living by fleecing unsuspecting strangers. The strategy was as old as gambling itself: make a great show of losing a few matches, push up the stakes and then nail your opponent with a final flourish, reach across the table and scoop all the money into your own pocket.

Hustlers could size up a punter in seconds, and they had a high opinion of their own skills. They'd offer their chosen victims a choice of sides, even the first move, in an effort to lure them into the game. When they weren't playing the innocent, these chancers were cocky, flamboyant and larger than life. They had cash to burn. To young Chan, who spent his hours pouring out tea and kowtowing to his father, their world seemed glamorous and exciting.

His father disapproved, but it wasn't long before Chan had picked up the game and was hustling for himself. He was bright, and quickly made a name for himself among the better players in the village, and then his confidence began to snowball. He was sharp enough to use his youth to draw in his prey, 'Come on brother, play again,' he would say with an insinuating smile. 'My tender years are no match for your experience and surely this beginner's luck must end on the next game?'

It never did, of course. Regulars would smirk to themselves as they heard Chan's trademark patter and draw around to watch his latest sucker take the bait. Chan called it 'throwing out a sprat to catch a mackerel', and he learned to reel them in one at a time.

His father watched anxiously. Chan was no longer under his

control; Fat Chow could see that his son had brains, resourceful-
ness and a good grasp of human nature, but he was using these
talents to tap into Chow's customers, not to better himself. He
tolerated the chess and it drew a crowd, but fights often broke out
over games, cheered on by the spectators, and it was Fat Chow who
had to break the battle up, grabbing both parties by the scruff of
their necks and tossing them out into the street.

If Chan was one of the men fighting, he was hurled on to the
muddy road too – Fat Chow made no allowance for his own son.
His attitude riled Chan, who was humiliated in front of the very
friends he was trying to impress, and the friction that had always
existed between father and son grew until they were becoming
more and more distant from one another.

Fat Chow was a traditional man who believed that the father
should be the head of the household – the absolute ruler. He
quoted the Chinese, 'A good ruler makes a good people. The prince
is the dish, the people are the water; if the dish is round, the water
is round, if the dish is square, the water will be square also.' He
wanted a son who would behave like the water. He would grow
into his father's image – well, maybe a little slimmer – and do right
by his parents.

Chan was heading in a different direction. His older cousin Yun
ran an illegal gambling den from his home in the village and Chan
began to drop by there when he could escape the restaurant, and
mingle with Yun's fascinating patrons with their dodgy connections
and seedy glamour. At Yun's place, unmarried men and women
could socialise, alcohol replaced the monotonous tea, and money

was wagered and lost in bigger sums than Chan dared stake on a chess game.

With his smooth talk, his nerve and his mother's good looks, Chan intrigued the ladies who met there to eye the gamblers, and he soon had a nice line in flattering little compliments to give them. He liked to flirt. This place, he thought, was his ticket to the adult world and out of the village.

His parents saw less and less of their son. He made new friends who knew Triad members in turn, and it was only a matter of time before my grandfather, dazzled by the allure of the pretty, dangerous women and the gangsters' edgy tales, joined his cousins in the Triad ranks.

Wherever the Chinese diaspora goes, the Triads go too. When my sisters and I were growing up in Manchester, we learned that the Triads were a fact of life. Everyone in the community knew who the local leaders were – we even played with their children and sat alongside them at Chinese school! We were all fed terrible stories of the revenge taken on those who crossed the Triads, and how the gangs had strange blood oaths that they swore to bind new members into the brotherhood.

Whether the details of these stories were true or not, I have no idea; they were certainly cautionary tales and Triad men became our bogeymen. If we misbehaved once too often, our parents would tell us that the Triads would hunt us down and carry us off. We were naughty children, but all I can say is that they never did burst in the door and bear us away, kicking and screaming.

The Triads were not always a criminal organisation. They began in the eighteenth century as freedom fighters recruited from the Hung clan to resist the invading Qing dynasty and bring the Han Chinese back to power. After nearly two centuries of living outside the law they were unable to go back to their old civilian lives, and formed a cultish group who turned eventually to crime and extortion to feed their brothers.

The term 'Triad' was coined by the Hong Kong government in the late 1940s to try to categorise the gangs that had flooded into the colony from the mainland along with all the other migrants fleeing the Communist revolution. They christened them for the triangular symbol that the gangs used, which had been used as emblems by the original secret societies.

My grandfather began his apprenticeship to the Triads as a runner for a local circle of racketeers. He joined a handful of children and young men who ran errands and fetched goods for the gangsters as they were too well known to risk showing their face out of doors in daylight hours.

Triad structure is very flexible, admitting or phasing out different individuals as it suits the organisation – it has none of the Mafia's family ties or rigid hierarchy. The ties that bound the men were loose, and Chan was not necessarily swearing himself into a lifetime of serious crime, but he was tapping into a privilege or two – rather like becoming a Freemason.

Different gangs had different focuses – some dedicated themselves only to criminal activities, others were like unions, or else little more than martial arts groups. The connections between the gangs were loose but they could materialise, linking a small rural group to an international fraternity of loose-knit individuals who might offer assistance or protection if it became necessary.

Membership was a matter of who you knew. Cut down to the most basic level, there was a tie between two members, the senior of whom was called 'big brother' or *Dai Lo* and the junior, 'little brother' or *Sai Lo*. The big brothers gave work, protection and advice to the little brothers, and they in turn gave their loyalty, support and a cut of their money in exchange.

To a small fish like Kwok Chan, the only thing that mattered was his *Dai Lo* and the way they got along – he could have had little idea of the bigger picture. He wanted to ingratiate himself with the local Triads and his *Dai Lo* encouraged that, praising him and confiding snippets of business to him, hinting at what might come if he worked well. He gave Chan a new bike as a gift, and my grandfather ran his errands proudly on the cherished machine.

He was about 17 when his *Dai Lo* first asked him to accompany him down river to Hong Kong; he said he had some urgent business to take care of, and needed Chan's help – an agreement had gone wrong. Nothing special. Chan leapt at the chance – he'd never left the village before, and the small-time activities of the Triads there hadn't given him reason to think that the game in Hong Kong might be played for higher stakes.

His *Dai Lo* only told him the name of the man they had to deal with and the address on the docks where he would be found – it was straightforward, he said, but whatever happened they must not get caught having their little chat with this associate.

Chan nodded, trying not to think about a recent incident. A

friend of his had been sent to steal money from a market trader by his *Dai Lo*, to test his nerve for the job. The stall sold woks so it was a good bet for a fat purse, as every Chinese home has one of the pans.

The boy took a hammer, planning to stun the stallholder and make a swift getaway with the cash, but the man saw him coming and knocked him clean off his feet with his fist, and went on battering him. The police came to collect the boy and took him back to the small jailhouse, where they beat him some more and branded his back with a red-hot wok to mark him as a thief.

When the boy was released, Chan barely recognised his friend – his face was black with bruising and swollen into a gross distortion of his features. This was the price you could pay if you got caught and Chan had no intention of letting that happen.

In 1931 Lily had already been in Hong Kong for six years, but for Chan, for all his swagger and bravado, it was the first time he had travelled so far from Guangzhou. The wind was up, and the little ferry churned and bobbed on the waves. Chan hid below deck for the whole voyage so that his *Dai Lo* wouldn't see him vomit, and he missed the entry into the harbour and the sight of the great ships and the mountains rising up out of the sea. He couldn't hear the noise of the quays over the thrum of the engine.

When he emerged from the cabin Hong Kong burst on him like a wave: the people, the soaring buildings, the noise, the smells, the frenzy... Chan stood on the deck like any slack-jawed newcomer – just the type that made Lily laugh so hard when she was a city girl. His *Dai Lo* creased up, rocking with laughter at the boy's incredulity. He seized Chan's arm and hauled him up the ladder on to the quay, steered him through the crowds and straight into a restaurant – a dimly lit, scruffy place with waxy table-cloths.

Chan recovered himself a little and began to feel more like a made man. His friend was important here. He had asked Chan to accompany him on this business. He knew the boss. He ordered the finest foods on the menu and plenty of wine.

That day Chan and the *Dai Lo* feasted on *char siu*, or 'fork roasted pork', choice pieces of pork seasoned with a mix of five spice powder, honey, soy sauce and rice wine, and roasted on a fork till it burns a sticky red and charred black. Chan ate raw oysters for the first time, straight from the sea, which puckered when he doused them with lemon juice and gulped them down.

His *Dai Lo* filled his glass, watched the boy drain it, then filled it again. He kept it topped up, watching as Chan, who had barely drunk a thing before that day, turned pink enough to clash with the *char siu*. Chan was deliriously happy. If only his parents could see him now! He was going places – this was surely the first of many such meals. This was life as it should be lived; he drank deeply.

By the time they left the restaurant, night had fallen. It was winter, and as the sun set the temperature had plummeted. Out on the quay the sea breeze had whipped up into something icy and sharp, cutting through Chan's shabby village clothes and chilling him to the core in an instant. A thick mist had rolled in across the harbour and settled over the emptying streets.

Hong Kong was in monochrome now, the market stalls had

been packed away for the night and the shops shuttered, the *dai pai dongs* had been wheeled away. The restaurants which were still open had their doors firmly pulled to, muffling the noise of the revellers inside. It seemed as if even the heavens had been lowered closer to the earth, boxing in Chan and his *Dai Lo* from above.

My family is not good at drinking alcohol. I giggle like a maniac after two glasses of wine and fall asleep after three. I know that Chan's face would have turned bright red because that's what happens to all of us – and I know that, having done his giggling in the restaurant, out on the cold streets Chan would now be groggy and thick-tongued, slowly slipping behind his *Dai Lo* and wishing he was at home in bed.

He couldn't keep track of the route they were taking, but the *Dai Lo* seemed to be heading towards the flotilla of boats moored off the quays out in the harbour, and his mood had shifted. In the restaurant the *Dai Lo* had been relaxed and indulgent, and now that he was getting down to the real business at hand he was terse and cold. He outlined the plan to the 17 year old weaving along behind him, and even if Chan could barely take his words on board, he knew from his tone that what was about to happen was very serious indeed, and that there would be no room for mistakes.

The pavement under his feet gave way to wooden planks, and Chan, who had been concentrating on putting one foot in front of the other, looked up to see that they were on a long jetty. Rows of junks and fishing boats were tied up along each side, bobbing with the current. Most were empty, the crews having long gone ashore to make the most of their leave, but a few were illuminated by a single dim lantern on the deck or in a cabin – perhaps lit by a night watchman or a sleeping crewman.

They stopped at one of the junks. Chan was told to remain on the jetty and keep watch – if anyone came, especially the police, he was to call out. Nothing should disturb the meeting. Chan decided not to ask what the meeting was about, and the *Dai Lo* did not volunteer the information. He had noticed that whenever the *Dai Lo* mentioned the name of the man on the junk, he grew angry. Now he gave orders to Chan in a quiet voice, but even the drunk boy could pick up the menace underlying it.

The *Dai Lo* slipped on to the junk and disappeared, leaving Chan on the jetty. The fog dulled the noise of the city, and his ears were filled with the sound of the waves lapping against the boats. He looked around nervously as the minutes passed, trying to ignore the fear gnawing at his belly. What if the *Dai Lo* didn't return? What if he was in trouble and Chan had to help him? He had no weapons. If the police came, would he just be frozen, unable to move, or would he have the courage to cry out?

Shifting uncomfortably on his frozen feet he pinched his cheeks to try and keep his mind focused. He must try and pull himself together. The sound of a violent argument broke the silence and he swung round towards the junk, straining his ears to try and make out what was being said – he could pick out his *Dai Lo*'s voice cursing, then a scuffle and a single sharp crack like a firecracker. The retort echoed around the harbour.

It passed through Chan like electricity, sobering him in one jolt and setting his heart hammering in his chest. Dry mouthed, he thought to himself that he knew what that noise really was – a gunshot. He strained his eyes into the gloom, and there came his *Dai Lo*, leaping off the junk and racing down the jetty, his feet pounding on the planking.

'Run!' cried his *Dai Lo* as he swept past him at full sprint, 'Run, boy!'

Chan saw the flash as the *Dai Lo* hurled his gun into the sea and heard the shout go up from the other boats – suddenly lamps were sparked all over the harbour and men were emerging on to the decks of the fishing boats. Chan turned on his heel and ran after his *Dai Lo*, hearing the alarm bell clanging frantically across the bay.

On the quayside he could see windows and doors flying open and the restaurants emptying on to the streets, people shouting and pointing. The wind roared in Chan's ears and his lungs seemed to be bursting already as the jetty flew under his feet – which way could he go? Hard on his *Dai Lo's* heels he jumped off on to another jetty that branched off at right angles and the tinny whine of whistles announced the arrival of the police.

Glancing over his shoulder he saw in a blur the men in blue uniform pouring down gangplanks on to the quay and heading for the jetties. He yelled to his *Dai Lo* in warning, turning in time to see that the other man had veered sharply away, and was now scrambling up a ladder before vanishing into the doorway of a large warehouse.

Chan was alone. He did not know Hong Kong or the layout of the wharves which seemed like some kind of maze to him now, and blindly he climbed the next ladder on to the quay and hared on, hugging a high wall on one side, scared to scale it and cross the street to try to lose himself in the warren of alleys in case someone grabbed him. He ran only into the space before him as it kept opening up. There was another gunshot, and a chunk of concrete exploded from the wall in a shower of powder.

The quay ended, leaving Chan teetering on its edge, sucking air into his burning lungs and desperately casting around for an escape route, his eyes watering so badly that he could hardly make anything out. Rearing up off the quay was an arched iron bridge so steep that in his frenzy he'd originally thought he could never climb it. Now he put his head down and ran full tilt up the incline, drawing strength from the very bottom of his being, numb with adrenalin.

As he reached the top of the bridge the energy was punched out of him at the sight of two men in dark uniforms racing up the other side with blunt-muzzled pistols, pointing at Chan's chest. He spun to see two more officers reaching the base of the bridge behind him and beginning to climb. He looked ahead and looked back again, his heart skittering uncontrollably. There was a way out.

His *Dai Lo's* words rang in his head, 'whatever you do – you must not get caught', and he had a brief, foolish flash of his friend's face after the police had beaten him, then he placed his shaking hands on the wooden rails of the bridge and leaned over. The bridge supports stood on small, rocky islets that chopped up the gleaming, black water into white surf as it swirled around. Chan's chest had begun to constrict.

He looked up to see the lights of Hong Kong as the officers began slowly to inch towards him from either side, holding out their lanterns and calling out to him to give himself up. Chan dug deep into himself and pressed his palms into the rail, hefting himself up on trembling arms. He thought of his father and mother and how stupid he had been, he thought of his friend and his blackened face, fear forced his hand. Whispering a silent prayer to his ancestors he found the last of his strength and levered himself up and over the rail and out into the night air.

I imagine him falling in silence. The bridge slips away from him and he feels as though he is floating, watches his hands paddling the air frantically as though they belong to somebody else, then his feet hit the water and instantaneously his entire body takes the impact of the drop. Pain, and the shock of the water which swallows him up, his mouth and eyes open to the sting of the salt as he tumbles down through the freezing black brine, dragged deeper and deeper by his own bodyweight. He wants so much to live, to see his mother and father and to apologise, and he sees his father's face looming in his mind's eye as he loses consciousness.

The police shone their lanterns down into the water, and called across to the officers who had just arrived on the quay to ask if they could see anything. There was no sign of Chan. Running down from the bridge to the pavement, they exchanged words, shaking their heads in disbelief – did you see that? Did he hit the rocks? Do you think he survived? He was crazy – like a trapped animal.

They knew the area – the bridge was high and the currents strong, the water raw. They decided to return to the spot with a boat the following morning to see if the body was caught somewhere underwater, and to watch for reports of bodies washed up further downstream. Then they turned for home and left Chan for dead.

They should have looked a little further under the bridge. Chan's prayers to his ancestors had paid off, and he had bobbed back up to the surface, buoyed by his clothes. As he fell they had ballooned with air, and now the water sealed his buttoned jacket to his skin, making a life-vest. A wave broke in his face and, spluttering sea water and coughing violently, Chan came to with a jolt, barely aware of anything other than the throbbing of his lungs and the queasy mix of alcohol, salt water and adrenalin.

He looked around him. The current was moving him quickly across the harbour and out towards the South China Sea. He cried out, uselessly, already too far from the shore to be heard. He tried to coax more strength from his limbs, kicking against the current and lashing out with his arms, but he was soon exhausted and further away from the lights of Hong Kong than he had been when he started. He was beginning to lose feeling in his hands and feet, and his face felt like a mask.

For a second time he felt his life-force slipping away from him, and he thought of the tale his mother had told him when he was a child, about the angels who watched over the young as they slept. He did not want to die alone. He prayed to the angels to save him. He prayed to be back in Guangzhou. For the second time he realised that he was sinking, sinking down to the bottom of the harbour.

Of all the tales my grandmother has told me about her life, the most extraordinary is her story of how she met my grandfather.

Cities make coincidences and Hong Kong provided the bizarre twist of fate that brought Lily and Chan together, the sea delivering him up to her.

My grandmother was 13 then, only a few months into her career as a junior amah – in fact she was in one of her first posts. Every morning she and Eva had arranged to walk together with the children they were minding, and the morning after Chan's ill-fated arrival in Hong Kong, she and Eva weren't strolling through the parks on the Mid-Levels but had been sent to get some fish for a dinner party that night.

It had to be fresh, the cook had stressed, with the eye still firm – they weren't to be fobbed off with anything that wasn't straight from the net. Lily and Eva went straight to the harbour instead of the market, being savvy enough to know that they could get something choice direct from the fishermen. The boats would be in as soon as the sun rose, and while most of the catch was creamed off by the big distributors who packed and sorted the fish in the huge warehouses on the sea front, some of the sailors preferred to do a little business on the side and make a quick profit selling a crate or two to passers-by.

Eva and Lily loved the excitement of this impromptu fish market, walking from stall to stall and trying to look like grown-up amahs who would strike a hard bargain while secretly marvelling at the spreads of silvery mackerel and herring, and the giant tuna, bigger than a wok. Squid lay collapsed in jellied piles, framed by oysters in the shell and inky-blue mussels and baskets of shrimp, still wriggling their whiskery antennae.

Once they'd selected their fish and Lily had had a chance to haggle the way her father had taught her, they walked back along the shore to take in the sea air and look out over the water and play their favourite game of wondering where the ships were going, and what life might be like in those exotic lands.

It was my grandmother who saw the thing lying in the surf first. She cried out to Eva who was in mid-sentence, and pointed to the water's edge. There was a dark shape, partially dug into the dirty grey sand, half in and half out of the water – a pile of dirty rags or a knot of rubbish. Eva didn't think it was worth investigating and didn't want to get her shoes dirty just to satisfy Lily's curiosity, so my grandmother left her behind, climbed over the small perimeter fence and picked her way across the sand to have a look.

As she got closer she realised to her horror that it was a man – a boy, even – the rags were his clothes, torn and clinging to his thin body. He was crusted with white sand and dried salt, and had a loop of seaweed around his waist. His hair was frozen into spikes and his skin grey. Lily picked up a piece of driftwood and approached the body. She gave it a tentative poke. There was no response.

Eva called out to her from the road, 'Is he breathing?' and Lily shrugged and turned back to the body, jabbing it once again. Still no movement. She circled the boy's body and crouched down by his face. Brushing a slick frond of hair from his eyes with her finger, she took a closer look at his purple lips and the bright red rims of his eyes. She knelt down in the sand and leant closer to listen for signs of life, and miraculously she heard the boy's faint breaths coming and going feebly.

She called out to Eva that he was alive, and Eva let out a hoot of triumph and rushed off to find help. Bracing herself, Lily rolled the boy over, and as he flopped on to his back his eyes sprang open in panic. He tried to sit up and dropped back against the beach. He felt as though the weight of the water was still on him, and that he needed to fight against it, but his muscles were torn and weak.

He twisted up and coughed up sea water, feeling life flooding back into his body and with it, pain. The blue morning sky was too bright for him and he shielded his eyes which were blurry with salt. He noticed the girl next to him, silhouetted against the sun, and as she leant closer, her features formed into a face. He thought she was beautiful.

This must be the angel he had prayed for. She was smiling and, as their eyes met for the first time, without thinking he smiled back. My grandmother flushed red and covered her mouth with her hand in embarrassment. Yes, this was truly the angel he had prayed for. She had saved him.

Suddenly there was a crowd around them – Eva had returned with some fishermen from the market and now they dragged the boy from the shallows as he groaned and spat up more water. They propped him against a rock and covered his shoulders with a grubby blanket snatched from one of the boats.

One offered Chan a canteen of water and as soon as the cool metal was held to his lips the boy drank hungrily, washing the bitter taste of the brine from his mouth. He could not follow what was being said. Another fisherman rubbed his back vigorously, a third tried to warm his hands.

A tall thin man in a headband squatted before Chan and asked him if he could remember what had happened, and Chan panicked and said haltingly that he had fallen from a boat. The group muttered in surprise and agreed that the water had been rough that morning. A few more men drifted over to see what was going on and a debate struck up about what to do with the boy.

He should be taken to the hospital. It looked like hypothermia, he should see a doctor – that they all agreed, but nobody stepped forward to hand over their hard-earned cash to pay for this waif. As they stood around the boy's soggy body the fishermen started to see the funny side of it, laughing that they should throw him back into the sea like any poor catch that wouldn't earn them any money.

The man in the bandana suggested that they inform the police, and at that Chan leapt into animated protest – there was no need to do that, he insisted, he would be all right in a few minutes. The fishermen raised their eyebrows and took a step or two back. This mystery was deepening. Most of them wanted nothing to do with the situation and besides that, they had fish to sell, but in fellow feeling for this boy who claimed to be a sailor, they didn't want to abandon him either.

A small voice piped up over the hubbub of the men's debate, and my grandmother announced that she would take the boy to her own home and nurse him. There was a round of coarse laughter from the fishermen, who had noticed Chan's nice looks and now put two and two together and came up with five. Lily flushed bright red and looked first at Kwok Chan and then at her feet. Then the leading fisherman shrugged and said she was welcome to him, and at that the crowd dispersed as quickly as it had formed, slapping each others' backs and imitating Lily's tone when she offered to take in the boy.

Of course, my grandmother did not take Kwok Chan home, Eva saw to that. She waited until the fishermen had disappeared from view and the three of them were left alone, then she let loose, scolding her loudly and at length. Eva made it clear that keeping the sick boy like he was some fat fish from the market was a stupid idea, and he was obviously in trouble with the police.

My grandmother was stubborn though, and said flatly that she had made up her mind – as indeed she had, she'd already started to have a fanciful idea or two about her new life with this dishy boy. The discussion broke down and soon they were at it tit for tat, arguing over Chan's head, and they were so carried away that it was only the sound of Chan's hacking cough that brought them up short and made them pause – Eva with her arms folded, Lily gazing at her good-looking catch.

Chan was still shivering uncontrollably with a chill that was now the beginnings of a fever. The girls crouched next to him again, trying to nurse him as best they could, Eva took his hands between hers for warmth and my grandmother stroked his hair to calm him.

My grandmother has always argued when she told this story that no one would dream of taking such care over a stranger nowadays. She is probably right. I believed her story, but it still seemed shocking that at 13 she knew she was drawn to a stranger so strongly that she wanted to take him home to her family. It was certainly an unusual way to meet a future husband.

Reality was beginning to break over her nice fantasies though, and my idealistic grandmother realised there was no way that she could take him home – she was too busy, and in any case her mother would never permit her to spend time alone with a single young man. Nice young Chinese girls did not pick up strangers at the docks and install them in the family home.

Kwok Chan was thinking too, as the girls' efforts to coddle him began to work. He could feel the gritty sand in his clothes and feel the sun's warmth on his face. He was lost and alone in a strange city without so much as the fare for the ferry ride home. His *Dai Lo* must be furious with him. The police might be looking for him, perhaps thinking he had fired the shot on the junk himself.

It was only a matter of time before the fishermen passed on the story of the discovery on the beach and word got back to the police, and they would come for him. He struggled to his feet, bowed his thanks to the girls and asked them where he could find the ferry to Guangzhou. Lily and Eva now lost all their nerve and started behaving like well-brought up young ladies. They were crippled with embarrassment and started giggling, looking at each other and at Chan and at each other again.

Chan realised with a sigh how young they were – they reminded him of his sister – and he obviously wasn't going to get any sense out of them, so with no real idea of what he was going to do, he turned to walk up the beach. Lily and Eva sobered up and, with a quick bit of negotiation, they pooled what little money they had and threw in the extra dollars they had been given for that morning's shopping. They could make up a story to explain it – they were trusted by the cook. It wasn't as though something like this happened every day.

Lily ran after Chan as he shuffled away, and flushing to the roots of her hair, thrust a handful of coins towards him and muttered something about 'breakfast', her eyes cast down. Chan took the money, and overwhelmed by the gesture, asked Lily what her name was.

Lily glanced back over her shoulder at Eva as though she was about to reveal some great secret, then whispered her name. Chan held her gaze, then repeated her name quietly, swearing to himself that he would not forget the kindness of the girl who had rescued him.

'My angel,' he said.

Lily turned to go to Eva, looking back once at the handsome young man as he stood on the quay in his ruined clothes and bare feet, and Chan watched her go, then turned towards the city. He made off into the streets, not knowing where he was going or what he would do. Lily and Eva made their way back to the Western world of the Peak.

Chan did not take the ferry back to Guangzhou that day, or the next. He stayed in the colony and began to make a life of sorts for himself, at first dipping in and out of the underworld to supplement what cash he could get by taking on the few menial jobs that were available. He didn't forget Lily, but as the years passed he didn't imagine he would meet her again – the chance that had brought them together the first time couldn't be expected to work again in the teeming city.

Eventually Chan found a steady job as a porter in the new Queen Mary Hospital in Pok Fu Lam, a valley at the base of Victoria Peak. He was in his mid-twenties and had grown up a great deal – he'd had his rebellious streak knocked out of him a little by a tough life in the backstreets of Hong Kong – and now he could appreciate the routine and the regular pay-cheque that came with his job. He was good at chatting to the patients, too.

When Tai Po was admitted to one of the wards to have a minor illness treated, she was taken with this charming young man who worked hard and with a perceptible dedication to his job. He wasn't rich, but this was the kind of man who would make a good match for Lily – he would see her right.

Tai Po had no idea that Chan and Lily had already met, though maybe that's not so improbable. After all, Lily would certainly never have told her mother that she had been down by the docks poking dead bodies with a stick, or talking to young men unchaperoned when she was supposed to be working – that would have been unthinkable – so when Tai Po invited the young porter to her home to meet Lily, she had no idea what she was stage-managing.

Lily didn't know what to expect when her mother told her to dress herself smartly to meet a new friend, and when the door to the little apartment opened and there stood Chan – older, it was true, but still clearly the handsome boy with the fine features that she had pulled from the harbour – she was struck dumb. Chan recognised her simultaneously and in shock, stumbled through a formal conversation with Tai Po and her daughter. Tai Po was puzzled but thought she might have done some pretty astute matchmaking – they were clearly smitten at first sight.

Over the following weeks, Chan became a regular visitor. He began to court my grandmother seriously, as Tai Po hovered in the background playing the good chaperone. At times the older lady seemed to be omnipresent, but sometimes the lovers could take some time to be alone and talk. Chinese society was changing, and even Tai Po could understand that there were new rules for courtship.

The young couple developed 'movie fever' and made regular trips to one or other of the little local cinemas in Wan Chai to watch the latest offerings from far-off Hollywood, sitting companionably in the darkness and holding hands. They joined the great and the good of the colony in a Sunday afternoon stroll round the Peak, and they talked endlessly. Not only were they from the same part of Guangzhou, but Chan had heard about Lily's family.

The story of Leung's death was a well-travelled tale, and of course Chan had heard the regulars talking about it at Fat Chow's restaurant. He understood why this beautiful girl had such an air of melancholy about her, and he prompted her gently to tell him about the murder. It all came out, haltingly, Leung's dedication, the way that the news was broken, the young Lily's guilt.

Listening to her story Chan felt protective. He could see how deeply she was still affected, and vowed that he would try to find out what had really happened and who had been responsible. It was the least he could do for his 'angel'.

Perhaps because she had lost her father so young, Lily felt a great mixture of emotions for Chan – she was soon in love with him, and she both wanted to protect him and to be protected by him. To her the significance of her father and of her new friend blurred, and she felt that although she had let Leung die, she had saved Chan, and that would redeem her.

In a short time they became inseparable, living for the hours they could snatch to spend together. My grandmother had never been in love before, and Chan was at once familiar and extraordinary, with his strange way of arriving in her life. To Chan, Lily seemed to have a Western style of acting and as she was still unmarried in her twenties, she had an independence that appealed to him. She was assertive, and outwardly at least, confident.

In classical Chinese culture love does not take this form – individual personalities and desires should be repressed so that parents and clan can put together the most effective partnership. Tai Po and Leung's love for one another was just a fortuitous side effect of their parents' ambitions: marriage did not mean love and love did not mean happiness. For most people marriage was a lottery, if you found yourself paired with someone you loved it was an unexpected bonus. As poet Xu Zhimo explained, 'Amidst the swirling sea of humanity, I shall seek the only companion of my soul; if I find her, I am lucky; if I find her not, such is my fate, that is all.'

Chan and Lily's romantic love went against all this; they were aiming for happiness – not exactly a priority of the Confucian marriage – and though Tai Po thought she had brought them together, the young couple knew something else was at work.

Chan was fond of comparing their relationship to the story of 'The Oil Peddler and Plum Flower'. In the folk-tale, a common oil peddler named Qin Zhong catches a glimpse of a famous courtesan called Plum Flower. He falls instantly in love, and while most men daren't approach her because of her great beauty and fine clothes, he is determined to win her affection.

He scrimps and saves his money for over a year so that he can entertain her in style, but when he has enticed her out to dine with him, Plum Flower drinks too much and passes out. Qin Zhong, patient even after his long year of waiting, sits quietly until she wakes. Poor Plum Flower comes to and retches, and Qin Zhong opens his robe to catch her vomit and shield her embarrassment.

His kind actions and patience win the beautiful courtesan's affections, even though she moved in the highest society and he was a mere travelling salesman. As Chan, who had never returned to his family home, saw it, his romance with Lily had overcome all social barriers, and he was proving himself as a gentleman worthy of her.

You may think it odd, but my grandmother never pressed Chan to tell her about the night before she met him – how he came to be floating in the harbour, and why he had been so scared of the police. He never offered to tell her. He kept all his connections to the underworld secret from her, and though she knows more now, she is still evasive on the subject. His tale was told to me by his relatives, and then only decades after he passed away.

Lily did say that Chan was still haunted by the terrible night when he had nearly died, going over it again and again in his mind

– when they were first married he would wake suddenly from a nightmare and lie awake, muttering under his breath that he should be dead. The mere memory of it would bring beads of cold sweat to his forehead, and he would put his hand to his throat, as though the water was flooding his lungs again, slowly suffocating him.

In the days of their courtship he believed he had changed and that his past was behind him – he would clean up his life and take the pedlar Qin Zhong as his model. Tai Po agreed without hesitation when he asked her for her daughter's hand in marriage.

The war created an enforced break in their engagement as my grandmother had to travel back and forth to Japan with the Van Houtens. Kwok Chan continued to work in the hospital, where he managed to get through the war safely. His wages may have ceased under Japanese rule, but he still had access to food and other supplies for barter.

In those terrible years, it was he who looked after Tai Po. Just as he had nursed her in hospital during her illness, now he made sure she wanted for little during the Japanese occupation. He visited her with food and chocolate, often after curfew and at great personal risk.

When the British forces recaptured Hong Kong on 30 August 1945, the city went wild. My grandfather and grandmother were reunited in the midst of a city-wide party, their devotion as strong as ever after their separation. They eventually married in 1946, and my grandmother and her new husband moved into Tai Po's apartment. Chan fell formally under the rule of his mother-in-law, Tai Po.

Chan's wedding gift to Lily was simple, but its worth lay beyond money – he gave her the answer to the riddle of her father's death. He had stumbled across some old friends from his Triad days in Guangzhou, and when they heard that he was going to marry Leung's daughter they broke their code of silence to tell him what had happened.

As suspected, Leung's refusal to sell out to Mr Wong had been taken as an insult, and his rival had started the fire that damaged the factory a short time before Leung's death. When Leung stubbornly refused to reconsider, Mr Wong had enlisted the services of a petty thief to vandalise the premises. He paid him with a few bowls of rice and a night with a prostitute.

Leung's entry into the factory had startled the thief who had panicked and struck out in fear. Leung's death had been a mistake. Tai Po's family did eventually bring Mr Wong to justice, and he was even briefly imprisoned, but justice in rural China was a luxury for the rich alone, and the merchant's family bribed local officials into releasing him.

The prosecution may have been in vain, but Chan's revelation let Lily lay to rest the demons that had plagued her for years. The guilt she had felt was lifted, and in her elation at being newly married, she fell even more in love with the husband who had given her this release from her past. They were looking out on to a new, open future together.

Their union was soon blessed with children – my uncle, Ah Dar, was born in 1947 and my mother, Bo Yee, followed in 1950. I've called my mother 'Mabel' in this book, and that is her name – the name she adopted when she arrived in England – but it's very common for people from Hong Kong to have two first names, one English and one Chinese. Ah Dar was known as Arthur when he came to the UK, and my grandmother's name was Sui King before she chose Lily for herself. Sometimes it's a practical choice – Chinese names don't trip off English tongues easily – although sometimes it's a kind of statement, as it was for Lily.

Lily returned to her work as an amah soon after the birth of each of her children, and it was after Mabel was born that she arrived at the Woodman's household. It was not considered desirable for employers to know about their amah's own family, and there was certainly no allowance made for servants who had children – they worked hours as long as their childless peers. They didn't think to protest either, as the work was well paid, reliable and still better than most jobs on offer in the colony.

Lily spent so much time with the Woodman's two children, and Mrs Woodman senior, that she became more or less their surrogate mother, while losing her own role as mother to her own small babies. She only saw Arthur and Mabel twice a week, and then only for a few minutes in the morning. One of Lily's sisters became their 'mother', while Tai Po did the bulk of the childrearing.

My grandmother earned the family's income, supporting them all – no child of hers would go to a silk factory or work in the fields year round, not if she could help it. It was a sacrifice, but she was building a better life for them.

She would save them delicious morsels of cake or broken biscuits from the Woodman's tea-table, and when she left for work early in the morning she would leave these treats, wrapped in wax-paper, on the kitchen table for the children to find when they woke. She made them clothes too, from scraps donated to her by the Woodmans. With a steady job and a husband she loved, a secure home and the blessing of children, these were happy years for Lily.

Her wish to work as an amah had been astute – Hong Kong's economy had been dealt a heavy blow by the war, and as it struggled to rebuild, a new wave of immigrants came in from the mainland, hiking up the competition for what jobs remained. Lily's husband was not so lucky in the post-war years.

He had little education or skills and soon lost his job at the hospital to someone who was prepared to do it for even less money. After that he could only find work fitfully, and spent a lot of time at home sharing the childcare duties with Tai Po.

Among the crowd of new arrivals to the colony were some friends from his home village who had retained their connections with the Triads. They were swiftly sucked into the underworld of casinos, brothels and opium dens that flourished in the Wan Chai slums. It was easy money, made by men who boasted of being their own bosses.

Chan slipped slowly back into his old habits with these friends, looking for a way to escape the humiliation of being relegated to nannying his children in his mother-in-law's home. Some nights he would return from the gambling halls flushed with success, money and alcohol, others he would be moody and withdrawn, and when my grandmother asked where the housekeeping money had gone he would ignore her.

She returned from long shifts at the Woodmans' to find her children crying and her husband gone. As she strove to advance herself in the Western world, Chan let the marriage crumble as he burrowed himself more deeply into the seamier side of Hong Kong. He blamed her as he wasted the money she earned.

Chan began to take his days off too, hanging around in dubious restaurants, lurking on street corners with the small-time gangsters from Guangzhou. My grandmother told me that much later she had discovered that her husband had fallen for another woman, a prostitute who introduced him to opium.

He had met her at a gambling parlour and they were soon thick as thieves. She became his accomplice, hoodwinking gullible punters at the mah-jong table – she was very smart, and Chan profited from the acquaintance. She wanted a way out of prostitution, but was hooked on opium. She and Chan fleeced gamblers with abandon, drinking freely and indulging in copious amounts of the drug as they fantasised about what they'd do with their winnings.

As their addictions began to consume them, they consumed their profits too, and Chan hoovered up every last penny that Lily made too. My grandmother could ill afford to underwrite Chan's new behaviour, but for all her independence of spirit she remained Chan's wife, and tradition dictated that she must obey him. The family went hungry; Lily brought more scraps from the Woodmans' table.

Chan laughed off her fears, and the more she tried to reason with him or argue with him, the less time he spent at home. Eventually he gave up any attempt to live at the apartment at all,

Leung's funeral, 1930. The village women are burning paper and incense. Tai Po is to the left of the woman with the white top.

Mabel, aged three, 1953.

From left to right: back row, Lily's oldest sister's son and youngest sister; *front row,* Mabel, Lily, Tai Po, Lily's oldest sister, Arthur. 1958.

Kwok Chan, aged about 36. This is the photo that now sits on Lily's mantelpiece.

Lily travelling from Hong Kong to the UK.

The last time Lily's family were together, on the docks in Hong Kong as Arthur and Mabel are about to leave, 1959. *From left to right*: A distant cousin, Arthur, Kwok Chan's sister, Ah Bing, Kwok Chan, Mabel and Lily.

Arthur, Mabel and Lily outside the first restaurant, Lung Fung. Middleton, UK, 1959.

Below: Kwok Chan's farewell party in Hong Kong, 1960. Kwok Chan is towards the left, with a black shirt and white tie.

Below: Lily in her red car, 1960s. *Below right:* Mabel, Lily and others, laughing and eating in Lung Fung, 1960s.

Eric and Mabel on
a date, 1974.

Eric, Lily and Mabel
peeling potatoes, 1975.

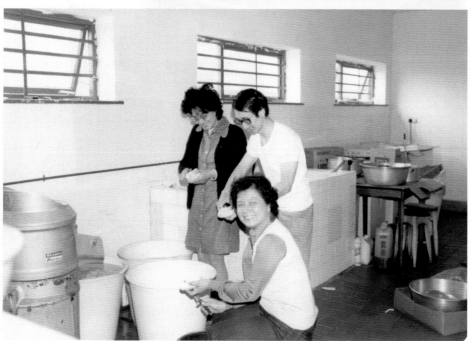

Me and Lisa, aged two.

Lisa, me, Jimmy and Janet outside the takeaway, 1990.

Our family trip to Hong Kong, at Wong Tai Sin temple. *From left to right:* Mabel, Eric, me, Janet, Lisa, our friend Yvonne and Jimmy, 2002.

My great grandparents, Leung and Tai Po's, house in the village near Guangzhou – still standing – visited by Lily's eldest sister. Note the two photos on the wall of Tai Po and Leung. Nothing has changed, locked away in time.

Below and right: Outside Sweet Mandarin on our launch night, 1 November 2004.

A family feast inside Sweet Mandarin.

Lily, aged 88, with a huge crab claw!

and returned only to empty the contents of her purse. It was no wonder that my grandmother would never talk about Chan, or that she had told us to stay away from the shrine she'd made for him. How could she have borne to love someone so deeply, and to have that love unpicked by one tiny betrayal after another, day after day. Even now, she remains heartbroken.

In the end she woke one morning to the sudden knowledge that the marriage she had poured so much of herself into, was over. Chan's behaviour had spiralled out of control, from weeks to months to years, and he had killed every last spark of affection and loyalty she had felt for him. She no longer cared what happened to him out in the backstreets; she only cared about herself and her children.

She cast about for a way to leave him, but she could see none. Tai Po was growing old, and despite her good job and reputation, Lily was broke, and Chinese society did not support or condone young women living on their own with their children. As the saying put it, having married a dog she must follow the dog, all the way to the gutter. It was her duty as a Chinese woman.

Chan started to come back to the apartment, but only to bring around friends to entertain, or even the other woman he was seeing. He had no interest in his children. When he came with the gang members or the prostitute, Lily would hide in her children's room and cry. This is what had become of their happy home.

One night when she returned home Chan was waiting for her, drunk on his feet, his pupils blown wide. He announced that the time had come for her to move out. It didn't matter that this was

Tai Po's apartment – somehow Chan had reasoned to himself that because he was the man of the house it belonged to him, and he wanted his family out so that he could move in his new woman in their place. Lily felt her knees buckle under her and she clasped her stomach. She had been moving as if in a dream for some days now, because in the middle of all this horror she had realised that she was pregnant for a third time.

When Lily told me this part of her story she broke down and cried silently; I had never seen her so distraught and desperately gave her a hug, trying to reassure her. In an instant she was cast back to that dark time, and felt all over again the fear and heartbreak that had struck her 50 years before. It seemed that time made no difference at all, and for all her years in England she was back in Wan Chai in the filthy apartment, feeling as though her world had ended.

She could not afford a third child, and Chan was certainly not going to snap to and become a father for it. She and the children would be homeless, and she wouldn't be able to work for the last months of the pregnancy – Mrs Woodman senior needed constant care now, and help with getting up.

A new amah would be hired to take her place and the family might like this one more than Lily. The choice lay between the baby and the job, but the baby could not be had without the job to pay for it, and Lily had no intention of risking a backstreet abortion – she knew enough from whispered rumours passed among the women in Wan Chai that many died from the procedure.

She put off telling the Woodmans until she could no longer

hide her condition, the black dress swelling too obviously. Summoning all her courage she asked them for a break of a few months, and almost fainted with relief when they assured her that not only could she take the time, but they wouldn't even think of taking someone else to replace her permanently.

They must have been baffled when she burst into tears and began to thank them so profusely – after all, she was a friend of the family now, and they had come to depend on her. They had no idea that this simple act of human kindness would mean so much in Lily's miserable life. This chance became the one fragment of hope that Lily could cling to in the difficult months ahead.

My grandmother gave birth to her third child late in 1953. It was a straightforward birth – a girl she named Ah Bing, and loved from the first, despite her desperate situation.

Lily had not worked for two months and had run out of money by the time Ah Bing arrived, and Chan was now running up debts in her name. My grandmother was reduced to begging in the street, Ah Bing slung from her back, so ashamed that she wanted to die.

In the end fate intervened and provided a blessed, but cruel relief. Lily had returned to the hospital where Ah Bing was born for a check-up and there she met a Mrs Lee, a petite middle-class Chinese lady with a fashionable hairstyle and immaculate clothes. She had recently had her appendix removed and was admitted to the hospital for a check-up.

Despite the age and class gap, she and Lily immediately hit it off, Mrs Lee commenting that she envied Lily her baby – she and her husband had tried for years and were desperate for a child, she did not feel like a whole woman because she had failed. My grand-mother laughed – who could be jealous of her ruined life? She poured out her heart to the older woman.

As they talked and talked, Lily watched the smartly dressed woman by her side, seeing how animated she became as she played with Ah Bing, and how warm she was to this complete stranger. In those few minutes she knew that she must give Ah Bing to this woman.

Her new-born girl would have a better life as a cherished only child in a comfortable home – what could Lily offer her on the streets of Wan Chai? A wastrel father and a mother who worked all the hours in the day to pay his debts. She made Mrs Lee her offer quickly, before she could change her mind.

All she asked, she said, was that she should be Ah Bing's aunt, and be allowed to visit her from time to time, and Mrs Lee, already enchanted by the baby, agreed immediately. She paid Lily's hospital costs and even tried to offer her more money, but my grandmother refused. They parted, both on the verge of tears – Mrs Lee in the knowledge that she would be a mother at last, Lily knowing both that she had done the most terrible thing and the only thing that she could.

True to her word, a few days later my grandmother paid a visit to Mrs Lee's home and wept as she handed over her beautiful, healthy daughter to a stranger. She felt as though her heart had been ripped from her chest. She was a traitor to her own flesh and blood, all over again, but she had had no choice.

Lily never forgot the baby she lost. She still sees Ah Bing in her dreams and wonders what she is doing, whether she is well, and what she remembers of her mother from the few brief weeks they spent together. Mrs Lee kept her side of the deal too, and over the years Lily paid many visits to her little girl and they exchanged gifts, and when Ah Bing was old enough to write, letters too.

When I was little I remember spying a pretty ruffled envelope with Chinese characters on it at my grandmother's house, and reaching out to pick it up, only for my grandmother to curtly tell me to put it down at once. 'It is not a toy. Do not mess around with my letters,' and I was stung – I had never heard her talk to me in that tone.

I found out later that the letter was indeed a special one, carrying a double bearing of good tidings and bittersweet emotions. Ah Bing was married to a handsome young man, and now she was expecting her first child. Lily had missed out on the most precious moments of her daughter's life. Time and distance do nothing to dull a mother's love.

She gave Ah Bing away to Mrs Lee shortly before Mr Woodman had called all the servants to the drawing-room of the house on Robinson Road and told them that the women in the family were returning to England. As he explained the family's itinerary and how much of the contents of the house would be packed into crates for shipping, Lily's mind was swimming with thoughts – how would she support her children and feed Chan's debts now? What would happen to them all?

Later that day when she sat over tea on the wide green lawn with Mrs Woodman senior, knitting as she listened to the old lady's tales of life in England. That's when Mrs Woodman made her offer. She had, she said, spoken to her son about it, and he agreed with her – Lily should come to England with them.

They knew, she added, that Lily had young children that she would have to leave behind, but that need only be a temporary measure – Lily would be travelling back and forth, and she could even bring her children to England in the end. She stopped short, startled by the tears that were rolling down her companion's face. Lily folded her hands together over her knitting to stop them trembling.

At a stroke she could be free of her cheating alcoholic husband. He could not go on sapping her strength and her wages when she was safely far away in England. She and the children could begin again, and in the meantime she could send money back to support them and their grandmother. Once again she faced the mountains in the story that Leung had told her all those years ago: it would take years to move them, but once they were gone her family would reap the rewards.

A few years' sacrifice would have to be endured once more, but what was that compared to the years she had already suffered, or to her future with Chan in the slums of Hong Kong? Then there was Ah Bing to think about. Mabel and Arthur could join her in England, but Ah Bing was now Mrs Lee's daughter and she would never be reunited with her birthmother.

Lily thanked Mrs Woodman and begged her to give her some time to think her offer through. The older lady assured her that they did not need an immediate answer, and that they would understand if she chose to stay behind. That night was the beginning of Lily's long debate with herself, and she ran over and over her choices. Finally she chose. She would travel to England with the Woodmans, leaving her children behind. To the Woodmans she was all gratitude – a gratitude that she truly felt – but inside she was steeling herself for the move. Lily Kwok was standing at the bottom of the mountain again, ready to begin work.

chapter six

LILY KWOK'S CHICKEN CURRY
SOMERSET AND MANCHESTER, UK 1950s

'Of all the stratagems, to know when to quit is the best'

三十六计 走为上

The move to England marked the beginning of a change in my grandmother's connection to the Woodmans. What was left of their master–servant relationship gave way to true friendship. It's a bond that lasts to this day, and every Christmas without fail she receives a card from them. Catherine, the little girl who was in her care when she first arrived as an amah, is now grown up and has her own family in Australia, and there's a card from her to match the one from England.

It was Mrs Woodman senior who represented the epitome of the Woodmans' open-hearted generosity to my grandmother. 'Mrs Woodman senior was like my angel on earth,' my grandmother told me once with a huge smile on her face, 'It was the blessing that changed my life and brought me to England. I have a lot to thank her for.'

That blessing happened rapidly once Lily had made her decision to leave Hong Kong – there was a bare fortnight left to transplant Mrs Woodman senior, the children and Mrs Woodman from the colony to their old home, and the packing task was daunting. Trunk after trunk of clothing had to be washed, pressed and folded for packing, and layered with tissue paper. They also had to sort the things they wanted to take home with them from the knick-knacks and pieces of furniture that could remain in Hong Kong with Mr Woodman. He was accompanying them on this trip, but would return in a few weeks.

When Lily prepared her own possessions for the journey it took her a few minutes at most – everything she had fitted into a single battered cardboard suitcase, even the new overcoat she had bought to shield her from the dreary English weather.

There were nights when she could not sleep as she was dogged by worries about what would happen to her children if she were not in Hong Kong to protect them. In the clear light of the morning she would know that her sisters and her mother would look after Arthur and Mabel well, and that she would see them when she travelled back to Hong Kong a handful of times every year, but that didn't calm Lily's nerves in the middle of the night – she found it hard to give up responsibility, having a mother's sense of obligation.

The Woodmans were sensitive to the conflict she felt and gave her the night off on the day before they departed, and that night Lily sat down with her family, minus Chan, to share a simple dinner. Over the rice bowls she looked her children in the eye and vowed to them that she would send for them as soon as she was established in England and had the money saved for their fares.

Arthur and Mabel were still too young to understand how long they would be apart from their mother, and they nodded solemnly, imagining that it would only be a few weeks before they saw her again. Lily knew different. It would be years before she could really be a mother to Arthur and Mabel, and her children would have grown and changed by the time she saw them in England.

Standing on the dockside the next morning she could think of little else. She gazed blankly at the huge white ocean-liner that would be her home for the next few weeks, with its single yellow funnel and tall, varnished wooden masts and shuddered nervously. This was the machine that would take her from her home and her family, and she hated it for that.

The SS *Canton* was one of P&O's workhorse liners, making the journey back and forth between Southampton and Hong Kong many times a year. It was over 150 yards long, 6 stories high and powered by huge steam turbine engines. The white paint was a leftover from the war – a reminder that the *Canton* had functioned as a hospital ship.

The dockside was crammed with people: sailors, passengers, well-wishers, and pedlars hawking goods, all jammed together in typical Hong Kong style. People pushed and shoved, chattered and made deals, they bought snacks cooked over makeshift grills set in steel barrels and sold from hastily erected stalls.

Hysterical women cried and hugged children while their husbands placed a reassuring arm around their shoulders. There were Westerners there too, decked out for the tropics with wide-brimmed hats and sun umbrellas. Detached and aloof, they stood a good head above everyone else as they moved slowly through the crowd behind their servants. Lily felt incredibly alone.

The Woodmans were travelling first class and my grandmother watched them as they boarded, their luggage carried up the wide first class gangplank ahead of them by Chinese porters in white and blue P&O uniforms. Another more formally dressed Western steward in a peaked cap met them on deck. He checked their ticket with a smile and summoned another porter to show them to their staterooms.

Once the first class passengers were safely on board it was the turn of tourist class, and they all scrambled up the ship's two smaller rear gangplanks like a columns of ants along a lolly-stick. Waiting for them at the end of the gangplanks were stewards who tore tickets stubs and ticked off reservations on sheaves of paper pinned to clipboards.

Above them, a pair of creaking cranes winched pallets piled high with luggage, freight and supplies into the ship's hold. Everywhere there were sailors barking orders at one another, making the final adjustments before the ship weighed anchor and pulled out of the port on its six-week journey to England.

It was time for Lily to board too, but she stood unmoving on the quay. When the ship's foghorn gave three long, low, deafening honks and the crowds cheered, she jumped like a school girl and fell against some of the other passengers on the side of the port, who laughed at her surprise. She must have looked quite a sight in her Sunday dress and her best shoes, clutching her throat and gasping for breath in shock.

The foghorn was the signal for all the remaining passengers to make their way up the gangplanks, so pulling her ticket from her pocket and picking up her suitcase, my grandmother hurried to the back of the tourist class queue, trying to hold back her tears. She kept glancing back over her shoulder, desperately scanning the faces in the crowd of well-wishers behind the barricades.

Among those faces – some weeping, some smiling and waving to their friends – she was looking for her children. She knew that they were at home with Tai Po, but she found herself wishing that Tai Po had brought them along despite her instructions, and that they were there for her to kiss for a final time. She craved the smell of the soft warmth of their hair once more.

In the early hours of that morning Lily had kissed Mabel and Arthur gently on the forehead as they lay in bed, and whispered, 'I love you. See you soon,' and smiled to hide her grief as she tucked them back under their thin sheets.

When she'd crept away and pulled across the curtain that separated their beds from the rest of the apartment, she found Tai Po waiting for her at the front door with the cardboard suitcase. She was crying silently, a steady flow of tears running down her cheeks. The two women faced each other, recognising without a word that they had each instinctively hidden their emotions to protect the young children.

My grandmother is still like that – she prefers to chatter or to scold you than to show emotion, and from her descriptions of her own mother I can picture Tai Po doing the same thing, trying to cover up her feelings by running through a long list of advice. Tai Po stammered on, covering everything from writing once a month to dressing warmly for the snow, and then Lily clung to her, not as the grown woman she had become but as the little girl she once was.

She knew that there was a tiny chance that she might not see Arthur and Mabel again, and she knew better still that there was a greater chance that she would never see her own mother again. She had made Tai Po promise, needlessly, that she would see that no harm came to her children, hugged her once more and stepped out into the street for the last time.

Now, high up on the steep-sided SS *Canton* her hands shook as she gave her ticket to the steward and he smiled at her reassuringly, then pointed to the heavy bulkhead door that lead below decks to the maze of corridors lined with tiny, Spartan cabins. Lily chose to linger by the ship's rail for a moment longer, checking the crowd once more for Arthur, Mabel and Tai Po.

The ship shuddered as its huge engines thundered to life and the final ropes were cast off. It began to pull slowly away from the dock, and both the crowds on the shore and the passengers crammed against the ship's railings cheered as they waved and blew kisses. The foghorn sounded again and hundreds of white streamers were released from the ship's upper decks, filling the air with rustling paper ribbons that spun, fluttering down the ship's sides and into Hong Kong harbour.

Overcome by her feelings, Lily turned her back to Hong Kong as it disappeared from view and plunged through the bulkhead door, clattering down the metal stairs with her cardboard suitcase in her hand. She followed the signs bolted to the wall in the narrow corridors and found her way to her little box of a cabin. Its door was still ajar, like the others on either side – most of the passengers were still on deck.

Her cubby-hole was decked out in P&O's chequer-board tourist class motif, and it was barely big enough for the cot that she would be sleeping in. A small porthole was punched into the wall, a few feet above the water-line, and there was a sink the size of a bowl in one corner with a small square of mirror above it, and opposite a shelf that functioned as a desk with a row of pegs for clothes above it in lieu of a wardrobe.

For the next six weeks, come rain or shine, storm or calm, this would be Lily's home. Lily slammed the door shut and twisted the lock, then she threw herself into the cot, buried her face in the pillow and cried her heart out.

When she looked up much later she was aware that all she could hear above the thrum of the engines was the sound of the sea dashing against the hull. She tossed and turned on the mattress until sleep finally overtook her.

She woke to pitch darkness and a storm, the waves swamping the view from her porthole, their crests white. The wind kept up a roar that drowned out the engines.

They were long out of the calm and safety of Hong Kong harbour and into the open seas. The ship had stabilisers to counter the roll of the waves but there was little they could do against the violence of the storm, and the *Canton* pitched and rolled up and down the swell. Lily's only experience in a boat was the short ferry ride from Guangzhou to Hong Kong and now in the dark she was totally disorientated, her head spinning. She vomited once, and a second time, and now that she had started she found she couldn't stop.

After an hour she was desperate, crawling from her bed to the sink and retching up the dregs of her stomach till there was nothing left, and she was dry heaving miserably. She decided in her bleary state that the sickness must be punishment for abandoning her children and that she must accept it.

She switched the light on, she switched the light off – nothing helped. She panicked, thinking that she would be helpless for the rest of the journey as she stood staring down the plughole of the filthy sink. Her groans were interrupted by the sound of a man whistling in the corridor – help at last! Maybe he could fetch a doctor.

She lurched towards the door and opened it to find the steward making his nightly round. She called out to him in English and begged him for help, 'I can't stop vomiting! I think the whole ship is spinning! I think I'm dying.' He took one look at her green face and laughed kindly, 'You're only sea sick,' he assured her, 'You should lie down, the storm will pass soon and then you'll feel much better, I promise.'

Lily staggered back to the cot and lay down, and before she could be surprised about how swiftly it happened, she fell asleep. She woke to daylight and a stab of hunger. The ship was now ploughing smoothly through gentle waves. She washed the sink and her face and dressed, then plucked up the courage to go and look for breakfast.

The SS *Canton* was a floating town in itself. There were shops and restaurants, a theatre, a hospital, lounges and day-rooms and the broad decks where passengers could stroll and drink cocktails. There was a badminton court too, and a sloshing swimming pool, and on a raised open deck at the stern you could whack golf balls into the wake, or have a pop at clay pigeon shooting.

The morning sunshine had brought out the passengers, a little groggy from the storm but eager to explore the boat from end to end. Couples promenaded arm in arm as children ran and screamed in excitement. Older folk lay wrapped in blankets on loungers, gossiping and taking in the sea air.

My grandmother did not see the Woodmans for long each day during the journey as she was not really allowed into their quarter of the ship. 'They were taken care of by the stewards,' she explained when I asked. A tourist class ticket did not include admission to the more opulent parts of the ship, but the Woodmans invited her over to the 'other side' and she saw the staterooms for herself.

She remembers the hardwood panelling and the glass in the doors and screens which was engraved in curlicues and stylised flowers, and the fashionable wicker chairs. The Woodmans' state-room was in first class, and positioned many decks above Lily's cabin, giving them a view of the ocean for miles on a clear day.

No expense was spared. They had a full social calendar to keep up with on this last bastion of true imperial luxury. They dined in black tie at the captain's invitation beneath immense chandeliers that clinked quietly as the boat rocked on the sea. Each night the seating plan was rotated so that the guests met and mingled with each other as they made their way through the ship's bottomless stores of champagne and gourmet food.

After dinner the central tables were removed, the lights dimmed, and the floor transformed into a ballroom with a 24-piece orchestra playing the popular hits of the day. They were waited on hand and foot and expected to see the journey not as a long slog back home, but as an extended holiday.

Every day Lily and Mrs Woodman senior took tea together in the first class lounge, but for the most part my grandmother stayed on her own deck in tourist class. There may not have been buffet tables groaning under the weight of lobster and caviar, but it was still the nicest place she'd ever stayed in. It was a holiday for her too, the first she had ever known, and her duties began and ended with taking tea with Mrs Woodman.

I like my lazy days – I need a weekend in front of the TV or two weeks in the sun with a trashy novel to break up the hard work and keep me sane, but time off has never interested my grandmother. I can't remember her taking so much as a long weekend off work, and even when she came to Hong Kong to see me she had set up a busy schedule of visits to old friends and relatives.

Now six weeks of idleness stretched out before her like the horizon itself, and she had to try to relax. There were staff to clean her cabin and cooks to serve her dinner – left to her own devices, what could she do with herself?

She spent hours wandering about the ship at first, and in the evening she joined her fellow passengers in the tourist class dining-hall where they made their own entertainment. One of the passengers played piano and another had brought a violin, and they held their own dances – a little more energetic than the first class formality.

Lily had never danced before but after she got over her initial shyness she took part with enthusiasm, if not with skill. She made new friends and learned to make small talk, finding out snippets about the diverse collection of people on board – it seemed as though all nationalities were represented there in tourist class.

She had a chance to see the world firsthand too, as the SS *Canton* made many stops to pick up supplies and drop off and board passengers. From Hong Kong they sailed to Malaysia, Singapore and the Indian coast, skirted the Arabian Peninsula and passed through the Suez Canal, then the Mediterranean and up the English Channel to Southampton. Whenever the ship stopped for a couple of days the passengers would crowd down the gangplanks to stretch their legs and take in the sights – Lily went too.

Her family was part of the scattered diaspora of Chinese people, so often she had relatives to visit, and she saw something of the life of the countries. What pricked her interest most was the food and the markets, and in the course of her journey she dipped in and out of kitchens across the world, looked and learned.

On board ship she befriended the cooking staff, who were also an international bunch. She found the rich food on the boat too much to stomach after her usual diet of rice, and so to kill time and to feed herself, she persuaded the cooks to let her use a small stove in their quarters to cook for herself. Soon she was cooking for them too. After a long shift in a hot, windowless kitchen none of them complained when she knocked together some dishes for them also.

It was on the SS *Canton* that my grandmother began to experiment with the new techniques and ingredients she found on her journey, and it was here that the dish that made her name as a restaurateur came to fruition: Lily Kwok's Chicken Curry.

Her elder sister Sui had married a Singaporean man and emigrated there, and from Sui's husband Lily learned to add a smooth coconut base to a curry. On the way to Malaysia she stirred in some self-raising flour to make it lighter and creamier, and in India she perfected the mix of spices that formed the hot core of the gravy.

By the time they arrived in Gibraltar it was approaching perfection, and the crew clamoured for her to serve it up every night. Lily planned the dish both to celebrate the journey and as a welcome home surprise for the Woodmans, as she knew they enjoyed spicy foods. She also served it to some other new friends she had made on the ship, Chinese women – some of them fellow amahs who were travelling to Britain with their Western employers.

These women became her surrogate family in her new home, a place where she knew no one. As my grandmother told me their stories I realised with a shock that she was talking about old family friends whose histories I had never known and could never have guessed.

The first of them shared her name with my grandmother, so on the SS *Canton* she became known as Auntie Lily to distinguish one from the other. She was much older than Lily, an elegant and classic beauty with high cheekbones and a willowy figure. Her mind was filled with memories of the grand embassy balls she had attended as a young woman with the rest of Hong Kong society, and she loved to dance – she moved like a ballerina next to my grandmother.

Auntie Lily had been married to a well-connected but largely unsuccessful businessman who had died leaving her and her daughter in some financial trouble. Auntie Lily found a solution though, setting to work as secretary to Mr Rothman of Rothman's Cigarettes, who had been an associate of her husband. Auntie Lily was good at her job, and as she worked her little girl played with the Chinese child that Rothman had adopted.

This easy life was shattered when Auntie Lily's daughter was hit by a car and died shortly afterwards, and Auntie Lily lost her mind for some time, crying uncontrollably. Rothman eventually had no option but to 'retire' her. Having lost her husband, child and job in a few short years and then struggled to carry on in Hong Kong for several more, she had decided that she needed to begin her life all over again, and boarded the *Canton* for England, hoping to leave her heartache behind.

She found a kindred spirit in my grandmother, who became her confidante and advisor. Lily made it her goal to help the older woman smile again, and she would egg her on to dress up in what finery they had and venture to the dancefloor in the evening, for Auntie Lily loved to dance.

They had long, lazy afternoons on the tourist deck lying on sun loungers, eating ice cream and talking of everything and anything until it grew dark. They had a passion for strawberry ice cream, in particular. In the course of their long chats they both realised that they each wanted to have their own business in England.

Just what form those businesses should take varied from day to day as neither woman really knew what England was actually like. They had spent so much time around the privileged British of Hong Kong that they could only imagine that the streets were paved with gold and that opportunities for wealth lay thick on the ground, waiting only for them to apply a little hard work. Perhaps Lily wasn't so naïve as to imagine a mansion for herself, but they knew it was true that many Chinese families had settled there and owned prosperous businesses – usually laundrettes. Now she and Auntie Lily pictured themselves scrubbing huge piles of laundry and it seemed a million miles away from their leisurely life on deck with the strawberry ice cream.

Lily also came across a woman called Kit Lee who was amah to a Scottish family, making her way to Edinburgh with them eventually. She was another beauty, deeply feminine in the way she carried herself, but with a striking cast to her features. To look at her you would not imagine that she could have a care in the world, as surely that sort of beauty was a passport to all kinds of blessings – queues of suitors, offers of support, magical worlds – but Kit Yee had a secret that tore her apart. She was a lesbian, and in 1950s' Hong Kong that was a scandalous admission that could ruin a life.

Kit Yee had risked all by falling in love with another woman who worked in a Hong Kong factory, and after they'd arranged to meet at a friend's apartment one afternoon they soon embarked on a love affair. In order to meet they had to spin all kinds of tales and use elaborate subterfuge – a good Chinese girl shouldn't be meeting a man unchaperoned, let alone sleeping with another woman – but

Kit Yee was so happy that she grew careless. Eventually her mother became suspicious and searched her room, uncovering a letter that Kit Yee was halfway through writing to her lover.

She was so disgusted that she threw Kit Yee out, vowing never to speak to her again. She informed the parents of the lover too, and they forced their daughter into a hastily arranged marriage to sever her link to Kit Yee once and for all. Heartbroken and disgraced, Kit Yee agreed to leave Hong Kong, trying to look on her exile as an escape from overbearing Chinese tradition.

Having led a double life for so long, Kit Yee was a complicated character, whose fear of being found out had mutated into an acute sense of paranoia. Lily learned very quickly that though Kit Yee meant well, she could not be relied on in a crisis – she'd developed a nose for trouble and she kept herself out of anything she thought might slide into a difficult situation.

When things went wrong she made herself scarce. Many years after they docked at Southampton, Kit Yee was working as a restaurant manager when considerable sums of money went missing from the business. The finger of blame was pointed at Kit Yee, and she slipped away once again rather than staying to tackle what had happened to the money.

My grandmother met Kit Yee and Auntie Lily at the mah-jong table – some people had brought mah-jong sets to while away the six weeks of the voyage, and the game rapidly became an SS *Canton* institution for the Chinese women on board. The first wall of tiles was clicked into place almost as soon as the boat left the harbour, and from then on the scene around the tables was lively and competitive.

Mah-jong is a classic Chinese game that enjoyed a huge surge in popularity in Hong Kong in the 1950s, particularly among women. It had been banned on the Chinese mainland in 1949 by the communist authorities, and now Hong Kong men began to grumble about doing the same thing in the colony – their wives spent so much time playing mah-jong that it interfered with their housework.

There are lots of hotly contested theories about the origins of mah-jong – one attributes its invention to Confucius, another to army officers and nobles in the mid-nineteenth century – and there have also been plenty of attempts to give the characters on the tiles some kind of philosophical or mystical significance. To me it always seemed like a Chinese version of gin rummy, simple to pick up yet hard to master.

There are many different variations, but the version I grew up with is played by four players with 144 bamboo tiles and a pair of dice. You score by forming groups of matching sets of tiles or runs of similar numbers, and the suits are archetypal Chinese emblems: dragons, flowers, the four winds. It might sound dull, but you need to be smart to play it, and calculate like a chess grandmaster, though luck counts too.

In Hong Kong it's played in huge halls, with hundreds of players seated round special steel-topped mah-jong tables, and they play so furiously and intensely that the room resonates to the clack of the tiles being thrown on the table. Of course, the Chinese give the game a little spice by placing money on it – you give the points a monetary value to suit the budget of the players, or their sense of risk. A single game of mah-jong played for high stakes can make or break a gambler.

My grandmother has an easy-going nature, but when she gets to the mah-jong table it's a different matter. Mah-jong is a serious business to Lily, and she'd learned a little about hustling from her husband, so she earned a little extra pocket money too. Lily Kwok was a lady of leisure at last, though she only really settled into this enforced freedom a day or so before the white cliffs of Dover loomed into view over the ship's railings. After six long weeks they had arrived in English waters.

Lily's first day on English soil was overcast and grey. When she heard the commotion of the docks in Southampton she had raced to the deck to see what England looked like up close, and she was horrified at what she saw. Now she laughs when she tells me how appalled she was – she looks back on Lily then and finds her horror comical – but this first sight of the seat of the Empire was a great disappointment to her.

The dishwater skies washed out the nondescript buildings, and though there were people going back and forth on the quays doing their business, Southampton had none of the dazzle and hubbub of the great Eastern ports. A flock of seagulls squawked and dived overhead, as if waiting to pick off the weaker passengers. To Lily it seemed to be empty.

A thin crowd had gathered on shore to greet the boat but they were not cheering and seemed to be dispersing before the *Canton* had even docked, as if they were needed to fill acres of space else-where. England was uncomfortably quiet. The passengers and crew of the boat called out jokily 'We're home!' as they shivered in the cold, or spat out a sarcastic 'Welcome to sunny England.'

Lily said nothing, thinking that now she was about to leave the *Canton*'s strange floating world and go ashore on this damp island, thousands of miles from her home, her children and her mother. She imagined that the drizzle was sinking right through her skin and into the marrow of her bones, settling a chill on her spirit.

Around her the English didn't seem concerned. They had wrapped themselves in woollen scarves and heavy coats, and now trundled down the gangplanks to greet their loved ones decorously. Some of them even managed a few awkward hugs before they broke off in embarrassed laughter. To Lily it seemed as though they were all standing in neat rows, their bodies held upright and rigid – and though she was used to the sight of a handful of English people behaving that way, she'd never seen so many of them, and there were no Chinese to rush around them manically and warm the scene.

After the initial excitement of the ship's arrival, everyone on the quay became even more subdued and she thought with a stab of homesickness about the quay at Wan Chai, where four times as many people would have been crushed into a quarter of the space, yammering and shoving and alive. England had all the animation of a morgue and it was just as cold.

Lily had already said goodbye to her Chinese friends and exchanged addresses; she had packed the battered suitcase and had nothing to collect from the hold, so she made her own way down the gangplank and began to look around for the Woodmans. She found them with the other first class passengers, pointing out their luggage from the neat rows of suitcases and trunks laid out on the dockside to two eager young stewards who doffed their caps and loaded them into the back of a taxi cab. The family cheered when they saw Lily and she found herself grinning from ear to ear, painfully glad to see some friendly and familiar faces.

As they waited for the baggage to be loaded, Lily tried to take in her surroundings. She peered through an open door in one of the dingy customs buildings and saw a woman on her knees, scrubbing the floor. She wore a flowery overall and a headscarf, and her skin was dark brown – not the deep tan that peasant farmers develop when they work through the summer, but deep brown like mahogany.

My grandmother had never seen anyone like her before – not even in Hong Kong had she seen a black woman – but what compounded her sense of strangeness was the sight of a Chinese woman climbing into the back of a long, shiny Rolls Royce. She wore a necklace of fat pearls that nestled into the soft fur collar of her beautifully tailored coat.

Presumably she was married to an Englishman, but her chauffeur was an Englishman too and Lily was stunned – in England everything she knew was turned upside-down, English people could be servants and Chinese ride in state in a motor car. This was not a world she knew, and she started to get the first inklings of just how she could change the course of her life.

The Woodmans' taxi took them to the railway station and they went on by train, with Lily sitting side by side with them in the compartment. She pressed her face up to the window and tried to take in the extraordinary English countryside with its miles of hedgerows, thatched cottages and small, boxy fields that were nothing like the rice fields she remembered from the village. It was all too immaculate, more like the parks on the Peak where she and Eva had walked, than true farmland.

'What do you think of England, Lily?' asked Mr Woodman above the clatter of the train.

My grandmother didn't want to seem naïve so she thought hard before she answered in all honesty, 'It's big.'

She blushed as the family laughed, and looked back out of the window at the overwhelming greenness that flashed by – it seemed endless. Hong Kong was a tiny nub of land, hemmed in by the sea and the Chinese border, but here there seemed to be no limits, only a rolling expanse of this peculiar scenery. Even now my grandmother is in awe of the English countryside – she likes to say that there are so many plants that it has to rain all the time in order for it all to stay lush and watered.

The Woodmans' home was a grand Georgian manor house that sat in a natural bowl between gently curving hills smack bang in the middle of the Somerset countryside. It had smart white window frames and a red-tiled roof that made it look like a giant doll's house.

Inside the rooms were high ceilinged and airy – half a dozen bedrooms upstairs, then on the lower floors a drawing-room with a blazing wood fire, a library with a little ladder on wheels for retrieving books, a long dark dining-room dominated by a polished table that ran almost the length of it and a hall tiled black and white like a chequer-board. Below stairs was a stone-flagged kitchen with a mighty iron stove as a centrepiece.

Life in Somerset was gentle and easy. After years of Hong Kong's weird intensity and crush, the Woodmans fell back into the wide open spaces of Somerset with relief, slotting back into their old life. Mr Woodman was well off, padded by the considerable sum of money he'd earned while working in Hong Kong.

He slipped immediately into a country life of drinks parties and dinners, pottering round his rose-garden, and getting in some hunting and fishing. Though he spent much of the next three years in Hong Kong and only retired to England in 1956, it seemed as though the time he spent in the colony barely disturbed the gentle pattern of life he knew in Somerset.

Lily on the other hand only knew a life where every inch was shared with others, and for her this huge manor and its sweeping grounds were lonely and even frightening. She lived for the brief trips they made back to her home – six long weeks on board another liner, followed by a month or so in Hong Kong when she snatched what time she could to see Tai Po and her children, then six weeks back to dreary England.

She didn't know what to do with herself in the Somerset house as there were already plenty of staff to keep it ticking over in a style that resembled but didn't match the protocol that she'd learned by rote all those years ago at the amah agency in Hong Kong. The children were either grown up or away at boarding school, and her duties with Mrs Woodman senior were light, after years of slaving in kitchens or polishing acres of wooden floors in the Western suburbs.

Letters from Hong Kong became her focus, and though Tai Po could barely read or write she posted mail to her daughter in England dutifully, even if it was just a scratchy drawing on blue airmail paper done by Mabel or Arthur, and signed in her broken handwriting.

In those first months in England Lily would wake every morning, dress hastily and run the length of the long drive to the box at the gate where the postman left the letters and eagerly break into it, searching for news from home. That postbox is the most vivid thing she remembers during her time in the house in Somerset.

Depression crept in, and Lily lost her focus. She didn't have a roster of tasks to scramble through, or the buzz of a city to buoy her up. She couldn't stroll to the market and pass the time of day with fellow amahs – the weekly journey to the market was made by car, and there were no Chinese women in the market town, let alone amahs. People looked at her strangely. The town was picturesque but stagnant, and Lily was viewed as an exotic oddity by the locals. Her mind returned again and again to her children, and she felt their absence like a dull ache.

She was grateful to the Woodmans and tried to put a brave face on things, telling them that yes, she had come to love their beautiful house and the gardens. In her heart of hearts she knew it had become a gilded cage for her, and she got no joy from realising that her suite of rooms was as big as Tai Po's entire flat in Wan Chai where her children lived among the grubby strings of laundry and piles of rubbish.

She ate good, regular meals, but with every mouthful she had to try and push away the thought that perhaps her children were not so well fed. She tried to throw herself into what work she did have, but the Woodmans no longer needed her local Hong Kong knowledge, and now she was reliant on them to explain the simplest things about her new country.

When she couldn't sleep she'd wait for the first light then wrap herself in a big dressing-gown and pace the corridors of the big house, stopping to stare out of the windows as fat drops of rain rolled down the glass, and found she couldn't focus on the scene outside. She looked to where she believed that Hong Kong lay. The days crawled by.

In the end my grandmother's limbo lasted for three years, which she endured with the same stoicism that she'd used to weather the silk factory and the years of polishing the floors of Robinson Road. She kept her mind on her children and as she seldom went out, she saved much of the generous salary that the Woodmans paid her, posting most of it back to Tai Po and storing a little every month in a biscuit tin under her bed. It would be a long time before she would have enough to make the return voyage and fetch her children once and for all, but she lived for the chance.

In 1956 Mr Woodman finished his work in Hong Kong and the house on Robinson Road was cleared. My grandmother was there to superintend the move, knowing that this time the family would have no more need to go back to the colony. She would be in England now until she chose to return to Hong Kong – if she could afford her ticket.

Lily was kept busy overseeing the men in brown overalls who swarmed through the rooms of the house, wrapping paintings and furniture in sackcloth and filling wooden crates with crockery and ornaments swaddled in newspaper. The family's many books stood in tall, swaying piles, waiting to be stowed. Not a single spoon could be left behind. In no time the Woodmans' house, which had been as much a home to Lily as her own grubby apartment, was an empty shell waiting for the next rich Western family to arrive.

The farewell to Tai Po, Arthur and Mabel that time was wrenching, almost more than she could bear. She boarded the liner to Southampton in a haze of tears, and spent much of the voyage in her cabin. When they reached England she was sunk in depression. It would be three years before she saw Mabel and Arthur again.

Her one great pleasure was her friendship with Mrs Woodman senior, which deepened over the years. They still chattered happily together at tea-time, and took gentle walks round the gardens, but Lily could see that her friend was growing more frail. When the old lady developed a hacking cough some two years after the last move from Hong Kong, Lily knew that she might not get better again – she had noticed that her friend's back and legs were giving her more trouble too, and now Mrs Woodman spent less time up and about, preferring her bed.

The doctor diagnosed pneumonia, but didn't rate her chances of making a recovery, and Lily had to face a new fear – losing her one true friend in England. To my grandmother, Mrs Woodman had become a family member and elder to whom she could look up, and she still honours her memory. She grows sombre when she talks about that kind Englishwoman's last days, and how one day when she knocked gently on the door of her room to wake the old lady after a nap, there was no friendly response.

Lily let herself quietly in and approached the bed. Mrs Woodman was very still and her skin was grey – she had passed away peacefully in her sleep. My grandmother's heart sank and her eyes filled with tears – she had lost a surrogate mother, the one who took a real interest in her as a person, and not just as a nanny.

Mrs Woodman had saved Lily from poverty and an abusive husband. She had given her a roof over her head, money to feed herself and now a chance to begin her life all over again in England. Lily took her death badly.

At the funeral Lily stood at the graveside along with the family, and listened to the sober words of the service as the vicar intoned them. Here there was another culture clash as the Woodmans wrestled with their grief, their English reserve winning out, and my grandmother wept like a child as the coffin was lowered into the ground.

When the family trooped sadly back to the house for the wake, Lily excused herself and went to her room, where she began to pack the old battered suitcase. She assumed that she had lost her job there and then – she had neither children nor Mrs Woodman senior to mind, so there was no reason for the family to go on paying her. She would have to make it back to Hong Kong as best she could.

She slept fitfully that night, racked alternately by grief for her friend, and worry about her own future and that of Mabel and Arthur. At 3 a.m. she gave up and switched on the little light on the bedside table, fished out the biscuit tin and began to count the money she had saved. When it all lay before her on the sheets she knew that it was a tidy sum, but not enough to begin a new life in England and ship her children over. It would, however, see her back to Hong Kong.

What would she do there? The agency would never employ a woman now passing into middle age with two dependent children. She would have to beg Kwok Chan to help her and the children, but for all she knew he had spiralled further into his addictions. Tai Po didn't report that he had shown any more interest in his children, or in Lily.

She gathered up the money and placed it back in the biscuit tin, thinking to herself that once again she had to brace herself for the worst. Then she pulled the covers up and lay back to try to sleep again, waiting for whatever the next day would bring.

She tried to avoid Mr Woodman the next day, though she knew he was looking for her. She wanted to hold off the inevitable for as long as she could, but he caught up with her when she was climbing quietly up the back stairs and briskly announced that he wanted her to accompany the family to the solicitors that afternoon. Lily nodded and felt a chill of dread.

A delicate mind can play tricks on anyone. I do not for one moment believe that the Woodmans would have discarded Lily – they were sincere in seeing her as one of the family, and in their deep mourning they were more than ever acutely aware of the way that Mrs Woodman senior had treasured her. Mr Woodman wanted to have Lily at the reading of the will because he had often spoken with his mother about what would happen to her.

That afternoon Mrs Woodman senior's will was read before her entire family in a small, wood-panelled office lined with books and ledgers. The solicitor was a stiff-looking gentleman with circular rimmed spectacles who had a habit of muttering his way through the complicated passages of legalese before suddenly declaiming the main points of the will so loudly that he made everyone jump.

Lily had no idea what he was talking about, even when he read out her name in his funny sharp voice, and Mr Woodman had to explain to her what had happened. Mrs Woodman senior had left her faithful amah a substantial sum as an acknowledgement of their long friendship. She had requested too that Lily must use the money to secure her future and to reunite herself with her children, whether in England or in Hong Kong.

When Lily finally comprehended just what the old lady had done for her she began to cry with abandon, the tension and uncertainty of the last week poured out of her as she understood that even in death Mrs Woodman senior had had her best interests at heart.

Like many who are born into poverty, to this day my grandmother finds it hard to understand how the old woman could have given away so much money so freely to someone who was no blood relative. It was only in the next few days when she talked to Mr Woodman that she started to understand how Mrs Woodman senior had felt about her. Lily had given her time, her compassion and her devotion to an old woman, even crossing the world in her service and leaving her own children behind. She had given Mrs Woodman senior a great gift of herself, and the Englishwoman repaid it now.

The rest of the family had not forgotten her kindness either, and now they offered her a home in Somerset in perpetuity, but in her heart Lily knew it was time to move on. Now she would finally begin her new life with her family by her side. She would go to Hong Kong and fetch Mabel and Arthur, and she would put her new financial independence into action.

Since her days accompanying her father with the little wooden cart through the Hong Kong streets she had had a dream that she'd hardly dared think of – she wanted to open her own restaurant and cook her own dishes in her own kitchen. Now she began to think seriously about everything that she had to put in place to bring her dream to reality.

She decided not to return to Hong Kong because she knew that she would be better off in England – there was more opportunity there for a woman working on her own, and besides, she could avoid Chan more easily when there was an ocean between them. England was still an alien country though, and she hated Somerset despite the Woodmans' kindness. She needed somewhere a little more like home.

True to her word, she had kept in touch with the friends she'd made on the SS *Canton*. Auntie Lily had a job as a secretary in a large insurance company and lived in Manchester, and Lily read her letters and descriptions of the city with interest. She thought that it was as good a place to live as any, and she knew that Auntie Lily had found a small Chinese community there. This is how my family ended up in Manchester.

She made a few reconnaissance trips north, camping on Auntie

Lily's floor. Auntie Lily showed her around the city and they pored over the property sections of the local papers together, looking for the ideal premises for my grandmother's restaurant.

In the *Manchester Evening News* they spotted an advertisement for an old shop in Middleton, eight miles outside the city, and Lily visited it the next day, assessing the bare rooms quickly and shrewdly. It was perfect, but the agent told her its price was £1900 – more than she could afford to spare.

She went to the one person in England whom she knew would have that kind of money – Mr Woodman – and pitched her idea. He didn't hesitate, but offered to act as guarantor to the bank for a mortgage of £1400, knowing that he had made a sound bet. He knew how hard Lily worked and how good her cooking was.

When Lily left Somerset for the last time the entire Woodman family came to the railway station to wave her off and wish her luck. She had served them far beyond the requirements of her job and now they had repaid her; very happily and completely mutually they went their separate ways.

In 1959 my grandmother honoured her promise to her children. Three years after she set sail for the last time and left them in Tai Po's care, she returned to Hong Kong to collect Mabel, now nine, and Arthur, now a grown boy of eleven.

The moment when Lily and the children left Hong Kong for England for the last time was captured in a rare photograph, now old and faded. It was the last time that the whole family came together. My grandmother keeps it in a drawer in the dining-room sideboard over which she placed Kwok Chan's shrine. It is framed but she never leaves it out on show – perhaps because she prefers to treasure it privately, or perhaps because it marks a farewell to the China she knew and the old ways she fought so hard to escape.

The family group stands on the dock in the shadow of another big, white ship. They are huddled together to fit into the picture, and their luggage is just visible in one corner, stacked in a small pile. Everything about the photograph is awkward, from the ill-fitting 'best' clothes that everyone has donned for the occasion to the forced jollity of the scene.

Even in a posed snapshot the family appears unused to each other's company. The children do not stand as close to Lily as they should; in the three years that they have been separated from her she had become something of a stranger, long imagined but blurred. There is trepidation in their eyes at the thought of the journey to come – neither has ever left Hong Kong. They are going far away from everything they know and everyone they love.

Ah Bing is there too, and she is six years old. She alone doesn't look concerned about the situation, but bright as a button and curious as to why she has been brought so hurriedly to the docks to bid farewell to a complete stranger. This woman is a ghost from her past yet also the key to her true self.

The children's father, Kwok Chan, is a stranger to them all. He has seen little of his son and daughters over the last six years, and is still living with the prostitute for whom he left Lily. He obviously feels he should be present at this send-off, but the role of father of the family clearly doesn't suit him. He looks pained to be sober in the bright morning sunlight, and it seems obvious to me that as soon as possible he'll be off to a bar to rectify this situation. He squints into the camera lens and stands crookedly, maybe thinking for once about what he has done, and how responsible he might well be for everything that is going on here.

The most striking person in the photo is my grandmother, beaming from ear to ear. Her smile is to show her strength, and to make it clear that she is bringing together all the pieces of her family that fate had tried to scatter. She is genuinely excited and optimistic about the future, but it's also true that she will not show fear, sadness or need in front of Kwok Chan – he is dead to her.

This photograph marks the beginning of our story in England. It is testimony to Lily's bravery and strength in overcoming her past and her drive for success in England. It is Leung's legacy and the start of our family's move to the next level, towards a better future and lasting prosperity.

Chapter Seven

LUNG FUNG

MANCHESTER, UK 1959–EARLY 1960S

'Don't open a shop, unless you like to smile'

没有金刚钻 别揽瓷器活

When Sweet Mandarin opened, my mother Mabel was on hand the whole time – she gave advice to my sisters and I, and mucked in to help with the hundreds of little problems that came up at the last minute and left us tearing out hair out. My grandmother stayed home to watch her beloved Chinese soap operas and left us to it. I couldn't blame her, but I also felt that despite the distance she kept she was also quietly happy to know that we were making our own way.

On the opening night I saw her sitting at a table at the back, watching us running back and forth from our guests to the kitchen and the office in a frenzy, and I realised that she was smiling broadly. I doubt she'd ever say it, but I think she was proud of us and of her own legacy. She knew what it meant to build something from nothing, and just how satisfying we would find it in the end when the restaurant was running to its own rhythm and the customers were flowing in.

She visits us there now and again, and she never criticises what we are doing or offers any advice. Instead we sit and talk about the restaurant trade as equals – she'll sympathise when an order is late, or a member of staff brings their personal problems to work, and it's reassuring that she knows exactly what we're going through.

My grandmother built up her first restaurant alone with no help from siblings or family, so no matter how hard my day has been it does me good to see her, because I know that whatever my problems are, they're nothing compared to her struggle to establish herself in a small northern town 40-odd years ago.

I grew up in Middleton and it's a safe, quiet place, full of good-hearted northerners. Our family's been there since Lily secured the mortgage on her restaurant with Mr Woodman's help. The town looked much the same then as it does now, its streets lined with red-brick Victorian terraced houses – now with new road signs and a TV aerial or two, but essentially the same.

In the late 1950s Middleton was known locally as the 'Holey City', a nickname it picked up in the Second World War when the Luftwaffe saw fit to pound it with ordinance – most of which never exploded. The story goes that the bombs had been made in slave labour camps and the workers had deliberately left out the detonators. When they fell on Middleton they didn't level the town, but just made big holes in the ground.

Middleton is 'home' to me and I love the way that very little happens quickly. Families stay at the same addresses and most people know each other by their Christian names. You could say it's because it's a working-class town, so nobody has the money to put on airs and graces, and when Lily first arrived the terraced houses were crammed with life. Extended families would share a single house, subdividing it into tiny flats, perhaps with 16 or more children between them. They shared the backyard and an outdoor loo, and there was a water supply on each landing for cooking, washing and drinking.

After the loneliness of her life at the big house in Somerset, I think the closeness of this new community must have appealed to Lily. It wasn't Wan Chai, but when she saw the children playing out in the street and the washing that was always strung out at the backs of the houses, the women stopping to gossip and the way people greeted each other in the street, she must have felt a little more at home. This was life as she knew it.

It took the town a while to get used to Lily, though. At first she was often mistaken for a Japanese immigrant, and got the brunt of the anti-Japanese feelings that still ran high, even more than a decade after the war was over. Some locals were suspicious of her, like the villagers in Somerset, and she had to try to explain where she was from and to reassure them.

The Chinese have been travelling to England for hundreds of years, arriving first as diplomats and traders in the seventeenth century. By the end of the nineteenth century enough sailors had settled in London to form the original 'Chinatown' in the Limehouse district, huddled round the docks. Emigration to the north began in earnest in 1948, when the British Nationality Act gave New Commonwealth citizens the right to live and work in the UK.

Nearly 50,000 Chinese people came to the UK in the 1950s, usually gathering in the great ports of London, Cardiff, Liverpool and later, cities like Manchester. Generally they built their communities in places that kept them close to the trade routes from China, and those who made the long journey did what they could to survive. Usually they began in the laundry business, then they switched to food, opening restaurants and wholesaling goods.

Though she wasn't far from Manchester, Lily didn't see much of her Chinese friends. The town was populated by white Christians, and Lily stuck out as a Buddhist Chinese woman without even a husband to look after her. Her English was still poor and the locals often wouldn't respond if she spoke to them in the street. When she entered a shop they stopped talking and stared. Of course no one offered to help when she started clearing out and repainting the restaurant.

All that Lily will say of this time is that she simply got on with doing what she had to do. She rose early and set to work scrubbing out every corner of the building, and at the end of a long day, when her eyes stung with fatigue and her hands were tender and swollen from being plunged into hot water repeatedly, she felt like the only Chinese woman in England. Perhaps it was too much to do on her own.

Manchester only developed a true 'Chinatown' in the 1960s, and Lily was the only Chinese person in Middleton in 1959. Eventually, by the late 1960s some other families arrived in the town, inspired by her success, and a small community was born. Now of course the Manchester area is a real mix of different ethnicities, and even in smaller towns like Middleton, Asians, Afro-Caribbeans, Eastern Europeans and Chinese are integrated into the community, but in Lily's day the cultural differences remained unbridged. She had to be an ambassador of sorts, as well as setting up and running her own business single-handedly.

The practicalities of opening a Chinese restaurant in Middleton were a challenge too. There were no Chinese supermarkets or wholesalers in Manchester and Lily's nearest source was Liverpool, over 30 miles away. The Chinese community there was in full swing, even boasting Chinese-speaking boarding houses for sailors who were in town, and there were shops that imported goods straight from home which arrived on the big cargo ships with the silk, cotton and wool from Shanghai.

You could get real Chinese greens too – *pak choi, gai lan, choi sum*; shipped over on the fast-plying cargo ships they could reach England in a week, but they were pricey treats and Lily had to learn to substitute English vegetables instead, carrots, lettuce, white onions and Savoy cabbage.

Rice came over from China in bulk though, as did bean sprouts, and she had to do her sums to work out the best margin. It rapidly became clear that she couldn't hope to lug a 20kg sack of rice back to Middleton on the train, so the sums had to take a car into consideration too.

She found a battered old Ford advertised in a local newspaper, and knowing nothing about cars, chose it because it was supposed to be red and in China red stands for good fortune. In reality it was brown and rusty, but that didn't trouble her. She taught herself to drive – a partial success, because she has never got the hang of changing gears.

When she'd brought the children to England to join her after a couple of months, she gave Arthur the job of tugging the gearstick this way and that while she handled the steering, lights and indicators. Luckily for her and for anyone else who ventured out on to the streets of Middleton, in those days there was very little traffic on the roads. Still, it endeared her to her new neighbours, who were highly amused. They could hear Lily approaching from miles off in the old Ford, gunning the engine and crunching the groaning gears.

There was no ceremony for the opening night at my grandmother's restaurant; she simply unlocked the door. She called it 'Lung Fung', which means dragon and phoenix – another harbinger of luck and prosperity – and it was a modest, converted terrace house in a street of back-to-backs. The windows facing the street front were wider, and there was a dining area at the back for sit-down diners and in later years, a takeaway counter at the front.

Lung Fung might have been Lily's first business but she already instinctively knew what was needed, and when my sisters and I sat down to plan Sweet Mandarin we had the restaurant in Middleton in mind. Lily made it a place that served its community, a place where the local builder, the priest and the policeman could share a table. The food must be good, the portions generous and the prices affordable – golden rules for anyone who wants to build up a customer base.

At Lung Fung, the locals could choose from a set menu with soup, a main course and a pudding for a bargain two shillings and nine pence. The soup was usually clear chicken broth, and the pudding was invariably ice cream, and maybe those are a little bland for today's sophisticated restaurant-goer, but for 1950s' Middleton it was perfect.

They framed a main course that was a choice of plain English – like a lamb chop and veg, or chicken and chips – or a Chinese dish like *chop suey* or *foo young*. Lily had developed a nice repertoire in the expat kitchens of Hong Kong, and she put both cuisines on the menu for Middleton, to let them make up their own minds.

She was sensible enough to recognise that it would take a while for British people who'd been raised on plain stews and boiled vegetables to venture a helping of spicy Chinese food, so she made special offers of the more adventurous dishes and kept on smiling.

Her very first customer was a window cleaner called Peter, and he didn't pay for his meal. He offered to clean the windows in return for a liver and chips with extra onions. With an eye for a bargain, my grandmother agreed and Lung Fung was in business.

Gradually she picked up some regulars who showed up at the same time on the same day every week and ordered the same meal. Soon she didn't even need to write down their order, but learned to shout out, 'The usual?' as they walked in through the door. The customer would nod and take their seat, enjoying the personal touch. Middleton got a taste for Chinese food too, and she found the Chinese half of the menu becoming more and more popular.

One of the converts was an ironmonger called John who liked a chicken curry, but insisted on having his portion of bean sprouts sautéed with soy sauce served separately. He liked them, but the thought of mixing the two threw him, so Lily dished it up specially for him. The first Christmas he gave her a box of chocolates and a bottle of wine, and he stayed loyal to the family for years.

During the war many of the women of the town had gone into the factories to work, and they'd kept up those jobs into the 1950s, liking the freedom it gave them, and the extra cash. At the end of a long working day they still had to feed their families though, and that meant preparing everything from scratch and cooking it on an old-fashioned blackleaded range that was a fag to light and clean. If Lily kept her prices down, the local women would get into the habit of nipping round to Lung Fung to splash out on a meal and escape their own kitchen.

For the hard-working women of Middleton, having a restaurant just around the corner where food could cooked for you, and there was no washing up to consider, was a godsend. Dining out was still a little luxury, but that was part of the appeal. Their husbands had the smoky dark pubs to go to after work, but there was no kind of social centre where the women could go to unwind, away from their children. That's how my grandmother's restaurant came into its own, and in no time it had its own nickname in town, 'Lil's'.

The dishes that Lily served turned out to be a big hit with the menfolk too. They loved the fire and the flavour of her curry dishes in particular. Most of them were manual labourers on building sites or worked in heavy industries, and their work was intensely physical. As the chief breadwinner, the father of the family was maintained and serviced like an engine – if he fell sick or got injured, the rest of the family would fail too – and he was after all the holder of the purse-strings too. The wives of Middleton kept their men well fed, happy and working hard, and stoked them with the occasional curry from Lung Fung.

In that first year Lung Fung meant nothing but hard work and isolation for my grandmother. She had a lunchtime and evening service to produce, raw ingredients to source, prepare and cook, tables to lay and clear, dishes to wash and a dining-room and kitchen to clean. The hours were long, and the cycle repeated itself day in and day out. As her children got older they could help out, but in the early days she worked largely alone, six days a week for fourteen hours at a time.

I split the management of Sweet Mandarin with my sisters but I still wind up exhausted and sick of work. Once when I was feeling low about it all I asked Lily how on earth she had kept going back then.

'You just do,' she replied unhelpfully, then added with a chuckle, 'On some nights I would see spots.'

'What do you mean, Pop?' I asked with a sigh.

'I'd work and work until I was so tired that I saw coloured spots on the wall,' she rummaged in her handbag and pulled out a spotted hanky, 'Just like these!'

It was a gruelling regime, and the locals noticed and came to respect her hard work. They also found a friend in her, and over time Lily became an agony aunt, a peacemaker, a matchmaker, spy and all-round shoulder to cry on. That took a toll too.

To add to her troubles, in 1960 a ghost from the past appeared on the doorstep – Kwok Chan. Lily's estranged husband had scraped together enough money to travel to England and now he arrived, a shadow of his former self, and clean broke. He was in no fit state to work, having been weakened by years of alcoholism, but he still showed up and placed himself in Lily's care, and she, like a good Chinese wife, took him in.

Perhaps he realised that he was very sick indeed, and he felt some remorse for the way he had treated his wife and children; whatever his motives, he wanted to be with them again, and he lived out the last months of his life in Middleton with his family. Having him there was barely better for Lily than being on her own, because he could contribute nothing and seemed to exist only as a reminder of the pain he had already caused her.

He died less than a year later and Lily buried him in England. This is the point at which she all but stopped mentioning him, as though she was trying to bury his memory too. Only when we shopped together, decades later, did she begin talking about him once more. And it was obvious that she had continued to love him, and that despite all that had happened, that chapter of her life had never truly ended.

In Middleton, money was tight despite the steady custom, and Lily needed every penny she could save to feed her children and keep up the payments on her mortgage. She determined that whenever people wanted to eat, Lung Fung would be open for them, and she didn't lock up till 3 a.m. on Fridays and Saturdays. Word got round fast – after all there were hardly any restaurants in the Greater

Manchester area that were open at that time of night, so Lung Fung soon got a place on the map.

Nightbirds stumbling out of house parties or nightclubs, or finishing their late shift, would turn up in the little dining-room for a hot curry and rice in the small hours of the morning. She gained a special branch of clientele that she couldn't have realised she'd attract – musicians and celebrities whose managers whisked them away from their gigs to enjoy a quiet meal away from their teenage fans.

The Hollies were regulars, and they relished the fact that nobody in Lung Fung made the slightest fuss over them. Little did they realise that Lily, far from being cool, simply had no idea who they were. There was one punter that she recognised though.

When Cliff Richard and the Shadows walked in and sat down, the entire restaurant was stunned into star-struck silence, then leapt towards his table to demand autographs. At the time Cliff was Britain's Elvis, and he and his band were the biggest act in the country. Mabel was a huge fan, so Lily knew a little about this handsome young man. My mother was beside herself to see Cliff eating a curry that she'd made herself, and nodding appreciatively as he tucked into it.

When Middleton found out that they'd had Cliff in their midst they started to turn up at Lil's in their droves to find out what was so special and to see if they could get a glimpse of their hero. It was all good business for Lily, and even if she didn't know who all of her guests were, she enjoyed their good humour and energy at that time of night – it made Middleton a little more like Hong Kong, perhaps.

On a high from their performances, the musicians would graffiti the menus with their band names and doodle all over the prices. Some of them made a sport out of trying to trick Lily into forgetting a few of the things they'd ordered, but mostly she was too smart for them.

Eventually she realised that one little gang was getting good at this, and making a sizeable gap between the balance of her books and the cash she had in hand. Fun was fun but now they were costing her money. She plotted her next move carefully.

Next time they came she put my mother out front to take their orders, and she observed them closely through the beaded curtain that hung between the kitchen and the dining-room. She could see that one of them was hiding behind the counter below Mabel's eye-level, and that he had ordered the same as one of his friends before ducking down.

She cooked the order then placed both plates of food out on the counter then went back to her place behind the curtain to watch. When Mabel turned away to get the drinks, Lily saw the young man reach up and try to grab the two plates and all hell let loose. Lily leapt like a Han warrior from behind the beaded curtain and the thief made a dash for the door.

They hared down the street, Lily's fury carrying her so fast that even though he was twice her size she'd caught up with him in 20 yards and jumped on to his back, then hung on like a cowboy on a bucking bronco for a good few minutes before he finally threw her off and escaped into the night.

Lily staggered back to Lung Fung cursing in Chinese and

ruefully rubbing her backside, only to find a roomful of customers staring at her open-mouthed. From then on the musicians thought twice before they tried to pull a fast one on the fierce dragon lady.

There was another side to the late-night crowd though, the beery men who rolled in when the pubs had closed and threw their weight around. Lily couldn't handle the volume of work that was coming in, and she was intimidated by some of the men. Wisely, she dipped into the community for help.

Mavis Brown lived two doors down from Lung Fung and she was a good-natured, cheery woman with pale skin and shocking blue eyes which she topped off with a helmet of peroxide blonde hair. She was as wide as she was tall, with rolls of fat round a waist that strained her blouse and gave her an imposing presence. She did not put up with any fooling around, but she had a certain rugged sex appeal too. She always wore flame-red lipstick and she never, ever stopped talking.

When she and Lily first met my grandmother could barely understand her. Mavis did not talk like the Woodmans. Not only was she never silent, but she was loud too, and she had a broad Lancashire accent and punctuated every sentence with 'D'ya knoor what I meeen luv?' even when she wasn't asking for an opinion. She was perfect for the job of waitress-cum-bouncer.

The customers loved her hospitality and good humour, and she was pragmatic and workmanlike enough for Lily to appreciate how she operated and let her get on with it. Mavis knew everyone and her presence ensured that Lung Fung became a hub of gossip and rumour. On her breaks she'd nip out into the road to have a cigarette and catch the ear of her friends as they passed by on their way to do their shopping.

She knew their kids too, and if any of them tried their hand at messing Lily around, it was Mavis who lifted them up by their shirt collars and tossed them out on to the street, yelling after them, 'I'll tell yer mam, yer lil' ragamuffin!' That was enough to sort out Middleton's teenage hard nuts. Mavis reigned supreme out front and Lily was the boss in the kitchen, and all went well at Lung Fung.

One night when she'd shut up shop and Mavis had disappeared home, Lily was standing in the kitchen chopping vegetables for the next day when she heard a knock at the door. She ignored it, too tired to bother with schlepping out to tell some drunk that he'd missed his chance for food. She picked up another cabbage and began to quarter it methodically.

Startled by a shuffling noise she looked up to see a dark figure filling the kitchen doorway. 'Your door's still open,' said a deep male voice, and Lily was so scared that she dropped the knife and sliced her own hand. The man stepped quickly into the light and she saw, to her relief that he was a policeman in uniform.

'I was checking the doors and yours was open,' he explained. 'When you didn't respond, I decided to check. I thought that Cliff Richard might be here having his supper.' He grinned sheepishly and Lily felt her shoulders drop in relief. The local police knew she was a lone woman running a late-night restaurant, and all their officers would check on her when they were out on their beat. This was the first time she had forgotten to lock the door.

She looked down and caught sight of the mess she'd made with the knife and almost fainted at the amount of blood. The policeman helped her bandage her hand and fetched her a glass of water.

'What did Cliff have to eat when he came here?' he asked again, as he pinned the bandage into place. There was still some food left over so Lily decided to show him. She fixed him a delicious curry which he shovelled down happily as she finished chopping the vegetables. A free meal was a small price to pay for the knowledge that the police were looking out for her, though as she said herself, she could do without losing a finger every time he dropped by.

A few weeks later this midnight feast paid dividends when she met the same officer again under rather different circumstances. She was out in the car on a supply run to Liverpool and, well, my grandmother has never really grasped the Highway Code. She bombed cheerfully round a roundabout in the wrong direction and found herself swerving to dodge cars that had had to slam on their breaks to avoid her. The drivers were furious, leaning on their horns and shaking their fists. She cursed back in Chinese, then heard the wail of a police siren behind her. For a second she thought about making a getaway, but the little Ford was no match for a police car. She pulled over and waited.

'Oh it's you again, Lily,' said the astonished policeman. 'Where on earth are you rushing to?'

'Sorry officer, am I driving too fast?' she inquired, blinking.

'You went around the roundabout the wrong way. That was very dangerous,' he said, trying to sound grave.

My grandmother bowed her head and mumbled to herself.

'But since it's you, Lily, and you serve such wonderful curry, let's forget about it. Now please drive carefully,' and with that the policeman got back into his car and drove off.

Bit by bit, so subtly that she could barely notice it as she rushed to keep the business ticking over, she was becoming part of Middleton, and the community was really warming to her. It wasn't until she was asked to prepare a Chinese feast as a retirement party for the owner of the local factory, Mr Smith, that she realised that Lung Fung had become something of a local institution.

Pleased to have been chosen for the party, she duly drove out to the factory in her little Ford to work out the details and parked the car haphazardly in the shadow of a vast, windowless brick building. Someone showed her in and she was on the factory floor once more, and disoriented by a flashback to her childhood in Guangzhou.

The noise and the heat generated by the clattering machines was overwhelming, the air hot and thick with particles of oil and dust. She felt her lungs contract and remembered the silk factory, and the steaming vats of water, and the way her hand had throbbed and blistered when it was scalded.

The factory in Middleton made cotton, and was a considerably more sophisticated operation than the sweaty silk workhouses in China. The ladies running the machines stood in rows, adjusting the knobs on the control panels with skill and smoothing the flow of the cotton. They all wore a uniform of matching white pinafores and small nylon hats to keep their hair tucked away. Some had found a box or a packing crate to use as a stool.

As Lily stood frozen to the spot, the foreman noticed her and came jogging out of his glass-walled office in the corner. He offered to take her on a quick tour, and Lily nodded in agreement, unable to say anything. As he ran her through the factory's routine she realised that conditions weren't much better here than back in China. To a woman who guarded her independence closely, it seemed as though humanity was sacrificed to productivity at every turn.

Everyone in the factory worked an eight-hour shift, and the women's working days were dictated to the minute. By the door there was a large clock and a device for workers to punch themselves on and off their shifts. If they were one minute late they were docked 15 minutes' pay. If they were 16 minutes late they lost half an hour's worth of wages.

The machines fired up at five minutes past six in the morning when the early shift arrived, and the clamour of the metal looms was raised as more workers joined the fray. They reached a crescendo at fives minutes to six in the evening and then the noise began to taper at 6 p.m. precisely. There was a whistle and the workers rushed to the changing room, tugging off their aprons as they went and desperate to be out of the factory and home.

The management reasoned that if a machine stopped, it was no longer making money, so the foremen were instructed to make a note of stoppages, and it wasn't uncommon for the weekly pay packets of 'repeat offenders' to be cut. The women hunched over the cotton, watching it closely as it flew between the roller and gears, and the foreman loomed behind them as they fumbled with heavy bobbins, growling at them to hurry as time was, after all, money.

The workers didn't need to glance up at the factory clock to know the time. The noise level and the frequency with which the bobbins were switched marked the hours of the day. They tottered home in the evenings with swollen feet and aching backs to start putting together the evening meal.

After Lily's tour and her meeting to organise the feast, the foreman showed her out. She stopped for a second by the door and looked back over the rows of thundering machines and sniffed the air. Cotton fibres tickled her nose and throat and made her eyes prick. There was a lump in her throat as she turned to leave, sniffing a little and wiping at her eyes. These women must have a party they would never forget, a real banquet. They deserved it.

It was the first time she had catered for such a big occasion, and she laid in supplies carefully. She fetched the huge surprise cake for Mr Smith, and concealed the box of presents that had been bought for him, and checked over the dining-room one more time. Everything was in place.

The women started to arrive, their hot, scratchy uniforms replaced with their best dresses and their most glamorous make-up. They were excited about the party and chattered away as they sat down to the meal, revelling in the luxury of having this spread of exotic food laid out for them. They drank a lot too, and the party went with a bang.

When the last dish had been cleared and the toasts were spinning out of control, Lily watched them all from the kitchen door and felt satisfied. She had done it in style. Somehow, too, what she'd done went some way to settling the ghosts of that factory in Guangzhou.

She thanked heaven that she worked in her own restaurant, and not at the mercy of a foreman with production targets.

She realised that Britain had given her an opportunity not just to climb the social ladder but to really make a difference to her adopted home. She may not have altogether integrated into British society, but she had found her place and she could use her restaurant to bring joy to its people. She knew that Mrs Woodman would have been proud of her.

Chapter Eight

MABEL'S CLAYPOT CHICKEN
MANCHESTER 1959–1974

'Better to light a candle than to curse the darkness'

与其诅咒黑暗 不如燃起蜡烛

*O*f course, Lily was not, strictly speaking, alone in the very early days of Lung Fung. She had my mother, Mabel, and my uncle, Arthur with her. The two children had to grow up fast – they were in a new, foreign country and they were flung head first into the frantic atmosphere of the restaurant where their mother worked long hours and it seemed as though the world was at stake.

My mother has often remarked to me that she lost her childhood innocence the day she arrived in England, and when I ask her about those years she's reluctant to go into detail. Ask her if she enjoyed her childhood and she will respond wearily, 'What childhood?' and then she'll change the subject rapidly or pull a goofy face to make light of it.

Mabel feels that she was made to work like an adult when she was still a child, and now that I know more about the way Lily was brought up, I can see why she saw nothing wrong with that. In many ways Lily's childhood was merely considered to be a period of growth that marked the time until she was physically strong enough to work. She thought that it was a family's duty to work together and believed that you were never too young to do your bit.

Lily would argue that Mabel had always been 'difficult'. There's a rather unsavoury Chinese tradition for childbirth, when the new mother is given a brew of pigs' trotters and eggs soaked in vinegar just after her child has been delivered. If the concoction turns sweet to the taste, the child would be sweet too. If it seemed spicy, the child would be short-tempered and hard to handle. Being deeply old-fashioned and superstitious, Tai Po made Lily down a cup of it after Mabel's birth. It was so spicy that she couldn't even finish it. The message was clear – this new baby was going to be trouble.

Family folklore had it that Mabel was a grouchy child. When she was a baby Tai Po could only stop her tantrums by feeding her lotus seeds and baby mice wine – another traditional remedy. When she grew up a little and realised what that comforting tincture had been made from, poor Mabel shrieked in disgust – like her mother she had a horror of mice. It seems to have done the trick though, as my mother grew up to be the gentlest, kindest of souls.

She was nine when Lily brought her to England, and she hated the country immediately, and Lily for bringing her there. She had been torn away from the only life she knew in Hong Kong and all her friends. She had been well cared for by Tai Po, who had effectively become her mother when Lily was out working for the Woodmans.

Lily had first disappeared then reappeared years later with little warning and uprooted her little girl. Mabel had no choice in the matter as she was transplanted to a polluted, cold and rain-soaked town in the north of England. She missed Tai Po's bedtime stories and her warm hugs. She missed her friends and the warm sun on her back. In the streets people spoke English in a thick accent she couldn't understand, not Cantonese.

They arrived on a dark winter afternoon. Mabel and Arthur climbed out of the taxi in front of Lung Fung and stood shivering in the street, while Lily unloaded their handful of bags and suit-cases. The children stared around them, trying to take in this unlikely promised land, and one by one all the residents of the street came out of their houses and stood on their doorsteps with their arms folded. They tutted and whispered to one another, 'First one Chinese, now two more. It's a bloody infestation! What is the world coming to? Did we fight a war for this?'

Mabel had no experience of racism – in Wan Chai she had been just another street kid, but now with so many eyes boring into her she could sense hostility mounting. Young as she was, she quickly understood just what it meant, as surely as if her new neighbours had run up and punched her in the face.

Lily's family were the only Chinese people in Middleton when she arrived and everyone knew who they were. Mabel was 'Lil's daughter' now. Her mother duly enrolled her at the local primary school and, as Arthur was dispatched to a secondary school a few miles away, she faced her first day in an English school alone. She tried to talk to the other children but she didn't speak much

English and her Chinese accent was so strong that they quickly lost patience with her. She was effectively mute, and they ignored her.

Her English improved rapidly and she finally made a small group of friends, but it wasn't enough to save her from bullies. She arrived home from school almost every day with her hair ruffled, her clothes torn and her eyes filled with tears. Lily was cut to the quick.

Chinese parenting techniques are very paradoxical. Lily would cover her fears by berating Mabel for coming home in such a state and for not standing up to her tormentors. Then she would make her a cup of tea, feed her lovingly and tuck her up in bed. As Mabel fell asleep, Lily would stand over her. For all that she had been through, she loved her children with her whole heart.

She would watch over her daughter as she drifted off to sleep, shaking her head in despair. It reminded her of her own struggles and sense of unease in this strange country, and the long years in the Woodmans' big house in Somerset. She, of all people, had known the same isolation and misery of trying to adapt to life in England. Mabel must have sensed that fellow feeling too in the tenderness with which that tea was offered, and the sheets were pulled up around her. My mother and grandmother are very close, and that mutual warmth is rooted in these decades of shared hardship.

The bullying did not let up. In the end, Lily caved in and decided that it would be safer for Mabel to return to the restaurant at lunchtime and avoid the playground altogether. She would be safe there, and my grandmother could keep an eye on her. She could help out too, because business was picking up and lunchtimes were hectic. Mabel found the work boring, but anything was better than school.

When the bell rang to signal the end of the morning's lessons Mabel would scoot out of the classroom and back across town to Lung Fung. She'd let herself in the back door, wrap an apron over her school uniform and get straight down to work. She carried plates, washed up and was in charge of adding the final garnishes to dishes before they went out to the customers.

My mother still finds the smells and sounds of a Chinese kitchen comforting. The long, unfriendly school day and the difficult lessons were broken up by an hour in the warmth and bustle of Lung Fung, the only tie that remained between her beloved old life in Hong Kong and this new grey one in Middleton. As Lily rewarded her with a big plate of steamed vegetables, she'd be transported back to Wan Chai, and she'd pick up her chopsticks with relish.

It's a tribute to my mother's extraordinary character and toughness that she didn't let these experiences get to the core of her. She has a forgiving heart and has learned not to be bitter.

Time made things easier; Mabel settled into a routine, the locals came to eat at Lung Fung and got used to the idea of having a Chinese family living among them. Lily and her children were generally polite so the neighbours left them alone – it's a British trait to tolerate anyone who can manage to say 'please' and 'thank you', no matter how different they might be. Mabel felt safe by Lily's side, and though she kept her distance she warmed a little to the hungry customers who enthusiastically tucked into her mother's food.

They came straight from the factories and the foundries still in their work clothes – boilersuits and flat caps. They spun their vowels out from 'No' to 'Noooor', and they had a whole series of peculiar but affectionate nicknames for Mabel: 'luv', 'chicken', 'doll', 'darling', 'princess' and 'sweetheart'. Lily piled their plates high and they wolfed it all down – Mabel barely had to scrape the dishes as they'd been wiped clean.

Downstairs in the restaurant it was cosy and lively at the same time, but behind the scenes there was only Lily's modest flat which sat over the dining-room. A set of narrow stairs led up to a landing with three small rooms leading off it, and stacked high against every wall were sacks of dry goods, boxes of extra equipment, crockery and cutlery. The smell of fried food and cigarettes drifted up and permeated everything. Lily had no spare cash for home improvements. The carpets were worn through and the dirty flock wallpaper was peeling. The floorboards creaked.

Mabel had a tiny box-room to herself, just large enough to hold a single bed with no space between it and the walls on either side. She would lie huddled under her blankets for warmth and stare at the cracks in the ceiling, wondering if she would ever see Hong Kong again. She still complains about the toilet in the old back-to-back.

If she woke in the night she'd lie and agonise over whether she really needed to pee or not, then give in with a sigh, pull back the warm bedclothes and race to bundle on a jumper and a thick wool dressing-gown before the chill could get to her. Then she'd have to dash out through the perpetual drizzle to the outhouse in the yard.

Once I wondered out loud if Middleton in the 1960s was all that much worse than the slums of Wan Chai, aside from the weather. She paused for a moment then explained, 'I didn't think England would look like this. I thought all the English people were millionaires. In Hong Kong, the English folk that we saw all lived in huge houses. I was told there were many such houses in England.' As she spoke she was looking out over the rows of tiled Middleton roofs from the comfort of her own home with its central heating and indoor toilet, 'I got that wrong.' Sometimes I think she has never really settled here.

In time Hong Kong became a dim and distant dream, and the experience of working in the restaurant curbed her shyness. She was in her element there, giggling as the customers called out, 'What's on table, Mabel?' and giving as good as she got – 'What? You again? Think this is your second home do you?' Like many bullied children she had developed a killer sense of humour, relentless and bone dry, which still helps her to put a spin on some of the worst things that have happened to her and leave a listener in stitches.

Lily's little family gradually became less of an oddity in the region as Manchester's Chinese population surged. New immigrants arrived to join the rebuilding of the city and the new airport ran flights to Hong Kong. With new Chinese workers came more Chinese food and restaurants, and soon there was a Chinatown to match, radiating out from Faulkner Street to form one of the largest Chinese communities in the world.

Rather than hire English staff, the restaurateurs flew in family members from the colony who'd work the long hours for lower wages. Like the Kwoks, many families ended up straddling the two continents, half in Hong Kong, half in England, often planning to return to the colony when they'd built a little financial security. Most had little or no formal education and didn't speak English, confining them to jobs as busboys and waiters.

By the 1970s Chinese food had evolved from an exotic delicacy to a cheap, regular indulgence, and takeaways and restaurants opened up in every city and town. The British palate was becoming more adventurous, and with every wave of immigrants came the chance to try a new cuisine – Greek, Indian and Italian all caught on, as well as Chinese.

Lily's business boomed, and she opened new takeaways in Bury and Blackburn which did a brisk trade in foil trays of sweet and sour pork and sticky white rice. She was kept busy shuttling back and forth around her little empire, and relied on Mabel increasingly to keep track of things at Lung Fung. She also called on Kit Yee and Auntie Lily to help out at evenings or weekends.

Kit Yee had left her amah job in Scotland and, driven by loneliness, come south to Manchester to be with the Chinese community there. Auntie Lily was still earning a living as a secretary but was happy to muck in at Lung Fung in her spare time. The kitchen rang to the sound of Cantonese jokes and wisecracks as the old friends set to work.

The cornerstone of Lily's menu at Lung Fung was the chicken curry that she had created on the long trip on the SS *Canton* from Hong Kong to England. Mabel served it in her takeaway when she began her own business, and we, Lily's granddaughters, serve it at

Sweet Mandarin. It's got something potent about it – I've heard customers wondering if it was laced with something or other that kept them hooked and coming back for more.

That makes me smile. I know Lily's chicken curry doesn't need any gimmicks – its principles are simple and its ingredients are well-sourced and those are the only foundations it needs. There's the aroma of the roasted garlic, onion and spices, and the sauce that's thick and creamy but still lets a taste of the meat through, even if beef has been substituted for chicken. The spices are hot enough to give it a bite, but its mood is hot, sweet and aromatic all at once.

It takes a day to make a big batch of the curry paste from scratch, and it involves the whole family. We make a week's worth every Monday, on the least busy day in the restaurant. It lasts longer now as we can use a freezer, but Lily would make it twice a week for Lung Fung. The recipe is a secret, and it's always put together carefully, beginning at 11 a.m. and finishing at 11 p.m., twelve hours later.

Mabel taught us. We would gather round a large steel saucepan as my mother ran us through the bowls of different spices, and then explained how to layer and cook the curry. The dish comes to life spice by spice, its scent deepening as it's stirred on the heat. We learned how the coconut powder is blended and softened to the taste, why self-raising flour works better than plain.

I can't begin to put a figure on the number of times Lily and Mabel must have gone through that routine, but every stage of it is honed to perfection. Periodically they dip pieces of bread into the simmering pot to check the flavour, and we would take turns to stir the curry into a thick paste. The smell drifts out into the restaurant.

At Lung Fung my mother said they'd always try to keep the fresh batch of curry for the evening sitting, but customers would catch the scent of it and batter on the kitchen door at lunchtime, demanding to know when the curry would be ready. It still has that effect. We put it on the menu at Sweet Mandarin almost as a sentimental gesture, but it's one of our bestsellers. I see my mother smile with quiet satisfaction every time she hears a customer order it.

My mother became a woman waiting the tables at Lung Fung. Her life followed an unchanging routine of school and work after school, at the weekends and in the holidays. She did well enough in the classroom but didn't follow her classmates into further exams or an office job. She already had steady work.

She was cooking as well as waitressing by then, and there was one particular dish that Lily taught her which she made her own. You cook Mabel's claypot chicken twice, first stir-frying meat that's been marinated in rice wine, then adding mushrooms and greens and baking it in the oven. In its claypot the chicken bubbles in a mixture of the marinade, oyster sauce and a seasoned stock, and grows succulent.

She cooked it for my sisters and me as children, and I know that when the lid of the claypot is whisked off, the aroma of the steam is glorious. We cook it now too as comfort food and for special family meals, sopping up the sauce with jasmine rice. It makes me hungry just to write about it.

When one of Lung Fung's old regulars stops me in the street to chat they'll always ask after my mother and tell me how they loved her like a daughter. She was accommodating and kind to a fault. She wore her hair in two small plaits and was petite and beautiful, an exotic-looking beauty in Middleton. No one had heard a Chinese girl speak English to them before, and she had the status of a glamorous neighbourhood novelty.

Her grasp of the language improved steadily and she practised on the customers, who didn't hold back from correcting her if she got it wrong. Today she doesn't have a trace of a Chinese accent, and she sounds 100 per cent British on the telephone. If you heard her you wouldn't guess that she was born in Hong Kong and spoke only Cantonese until she was nine.

My sisters and I grew up speaking English, and we were barely aware of ourselves as 'different' to our white schoolmates. We were born here and we share all kinds of culture with our friends, we can reminisce about TV programmes or books we've read or what we did at school. My mother had a foot in both camps, and by the time she was a teenager she was just as eager a consumer of pop music and cinema as the other girls at school.

There was a small radio on the counter at Lung Fung and whenever the Beatles came on Mabel would turn up the volume and dance. She devoured teenage magazines too, and she lapped up all the fan material on her favourite group – she was besotted by the Fab Four, and she even managed to go and see them at the Co-op Hall in Long Street in 1963. She goes a little misty eyed when she remembers the atmosphere and the way the music was drowned out by the screams of 300 girls packed into the tiny hall. Feverish with excitement, she screamed along with them, barely able to believe that the real John, Paul, George and Ringo were right there in front of her.

By the time she was in her late teens she had been working at Lung Fung for nearly a decade. While her older brother Arthur talked incessantly about getting out of the restaurant and getting away from Middleton, Mabel was less ambitious – she couldn't see anything changing. She did hope to get married, but for now didn't imagine having much more from life than she already had.

One day when she was 18 she was lolling about on her bed reading magazines when Lily called for her. My grandmother told her that her auntie and uncle were coming to stay, and that she needed Mabel to go to Manchester airport to pick them up. She couldn't take time off herself, and her sister and brother-in-law had never set foot in England before.

They were stopping over en route to Canada, where they were hoping to start a business of their own. They would be accompanied by a young man called Eric, or Shu, who had some catering experience and was going to work for them once they got there.

Eric came from the same area of China as Mabel's family, a tiny village outside Guangzhou. The Tse clan controlled the village, and the bulk of their income came from manufacturing a local speciality, a sweet and sour sauce. Like many of the villagers, Eric's surname was shared with the ruling clan – for centuries peasant people had not travelled far and so in some shape or form they were all distantly related.

The story of Eric's family traced a similar course to Mabel's. They had left the village for Hong Kong, and in the mid-1960s Eric's father worked at the upmarket Mandarin Oriental hotel. He learned to cook a westernised oriental cuisine there, and he taught his son in turn.

Eric was the oldest of six, and like any Chinese son he grew up burdened with plenty of responsibilities and the lion's share of his parents' expectations. He felt as though he was expected to have no future other than trudging in his father's footsteps in the food business, but he wanted a little more out of life. He loved all things Western – the movies, the music – and as teenager he was a sort of Hong Kong mod, with shaggy hair and thick black glasses.

By the 1970s he needed a way out of the stifling family pressures that had been building since he was born, and he settled on emigrating to Canada on a whim. Some of his more adventurous friends had already left the colony for North America, and they were writing back with thrilling tales of how they lived in mansions and drove big cars.

His own tiny flat seemed to shrink when he read the letters from his friends, and his family loomed larger, fighting and nagging him, telling him what to do. He knew Hong Kong and he thought he knew how he'd end up if he stayed there – maybe with his own family, crammed in another little apartment like his parents and brothers and sisters. The wide-open spaces of Canada began to take form in his mind. That, surely, was a sure-fire ticket to the good life.

He started asking around. He told a few friends about his plans for Canada and they told some other friends, and it jogged someone else's memory, and so he was introduced to my great-uncle who was looking for people to work for him in Canada. Eric signed up with him, bringing his family's sweet and sour sauce recipe as part of the bargain. This was where his new life began.

Well, almost. It turned out that Eric's new life took on an unexpected twist. When they landed at Manchester my great-uncle guided his wife and Eric through customs and out into the arrivals lounge, and straight to the woman who would become the love of his life.

The way my father likes to tell it, the instant he first laid eyes on my mother, waiting patiently at the arrival gate with her clear skin and her fashionable Western clothes, he fell head over heels in love. When she tentatively said hello, he had more or less decided that he would stay in England. My mother was bowled over too, but she tried not to show it, greeting her aunt and uncle and leading everyone out to the car.

When Dad goes on with the story, he skips straight to his first date with Mabel in Manchester, and tries to make my mother blush by recalling how he proposed and she thought he must be joking so she ignored him outright. He had to go on proposing for weeks before she took him seriously. 'I knew I would marry her from the moment I saw her,' he likes to say, and I don't think he ever doubted that spontaneous decision, for all the ups and downs they've had together.

Neither of them had had much experience of love or romance before they met. Mabel's life revolved round waiting tables in Lung Fung, and she couldn't picture herself as the object of someone's romantic passion, let alone as wife material. Her innocence meant that she fell for Eric fast and hard. Like her mother before her,

Mabel would be lucky enough to marry for love. At first they did not tell Lily what had happened.

Instead, Eric asked Lily if he could stay on and work at Lung Fung as he had changed his mind about travelling to Canada. Answering as a businesswoman rather than as a mother, Lily agreed to take him on. He was a skilled Chinese chef and, she reasoned, cheap labour – something she desperately needed to keep the two takeaways and Lung Fung running smoothly. Her jovial and ambitious son Arthur was leaving Middleton to join another uncle in Bristol, and this young man could take his place. Eric was soon installed in the kitchen at Lung Fung making batches of his sweet and sour sauce.

It was a cosy set-up in the tiny flat, perhaps a bit too cosy for Lily, who soon realised that she couldn't ignore the way that Mabel was falling in love with Eric. She felt ousted, an outsider in her own home. Eric was making inroads in both her beloved family and her business.

She had trouble accepting that the little girl whom she had fought so hard to feed and clothe and bring to England was now a grown up who was going to decide her own destiny. She hated the fact that she could do nothing to stop the relationship from blossoming, so she half-heartedly turned a blind eye, rationalising that it wasn't as though there were any other young Chinese men in Middleton for Mabel to meet.

My mother was in a daze. She found Eric both exotic after the Middleton crowd and familiar at the same time – they could talk for hours about the Hong Kong she had had to leave behind as a child. He charmed her with teasing jokes and compliments, and he bought a car of his own so he could take her to the cinema on their nights off. All at once she had the excitement and the attention that she'd been craving for years, and here was this handsome young man, totally besotted with her.

They talked about the foods they missed, pigs' trotters in vinegar or ducks' feet with black beans and bean curd. They laughed about the baby mice rice wine and snake blood, which sent shivers down the spines of Westerners. They spoke about being Chinese and what it meant in Britain, whether the old Chinese rituals needed to be continued in the West, and swapped stupid mistakes and puns they'd made by fudging Chinese and English words. My mother could not have talked about such things with her English friends – they would not have understood. With Eric, she felt at ease and was relaxed, and he was fun and full of energy. He had a very bawdy sense of humour, and he was eager to please her.

For the first time, my mother did not feel that her identity belonged to a place that was thousands of miles away. Now it was right in front of her. Eric was proud of his Chinese ancestry, but he argued with a passion that you could be Chinese without being bound into living out every tradition like an obligation.

As he put it to Mabel, you could carry your Chinese identity around with you like a bag, wherever you went in the world. Sometimes you're happy just to carry it like a security blanket, sometimes you might rummage in it to try to find something you thought was there. Sometimes you would draw things from it for use with care and respect, and pack them carefully back when you were done. Sometimes you just left it in a safe place for another day.

My mother, who had never seen further than Lung Fung before, now started to think big. Eric was a dreamer, and hungry for success and the money it brings. He had plenty of plans and my mother was all to ready to believe them, and picture the two of them leaving Middleton and travelling the world.

He made her feel comfortable in her own skin, and they found their own way to ride two horses at once, Chinese and English. My sisters and I grew up in that one-family melting-pot.

This was all some years ahead though, and there were a few obstacles to overcome first. My mother, for all her infatuation, was caught between an obligation to her mother, who had sacrificed so much for her, and the heady new plans that Eric was stewing. He wanted them to leave Lung Fung and set up on their own.

Lily, who didn't know this, was talking about expanding the restaurant and giving Mabel more responsibility. Mabel was caught between love and loyalty; her dedication to Lily had been unswerving till this point, but now she had Eric, and he had changed the way she saw everything. Torn with indecision and racked with guilt, my mother decided to leave the tiny flat and Lung Fung and Lily's reign, and build up her own business with the man she loved, my father, Eric.

chapter nine

CHIPS, CHIPS, CHIPS
MANCHESTER 1975–2003

'Unless we change direction, we are likely to wind up where we are headed'

除非我们改变方向 我们都会按照既定的路线走下去

*W*hen they went hand in hand to Lily and told her that they were engaged, Lily smiled on them, but she sighed inwardly too. She made it clear that she felt that she was losing her daughter – her little girl had grown up overnight – but she consoled herself that Eric was at least Chinese, and a good honest man. He was in the food business too, so he wouldn't be taking her beloved daughter very far.

My parents were married in 1975 in a small traditional ceremony in Bury. They tell me it was a fine day but there are no photos to mark the occasion because the photographer opened his camera too soon and exposed the reel. My father and mother hardly knew each other, and were very young to be taking such a huge step, but they took it fearlessly.

They didn't have a honeymoon and the routine of the restaurant continued largely uninterrupted: my father continued to cook and assist at the wok and my mother dealt with customers. There were a couple of small domestic rearrangements upstairs as my father moved into Mabel's tiny room with his few possessions. For the time being they kept quiet about their plans to set up on their own, and life in the little flat was tolerable, but space was tight and Lily was the matriarch and Eric was obliged to obey her.

Like any new son-in-law, my father sought her approval, keen to ingratiate himself into his new mother-in-law's affections. He suggested new dishes and methods to improve efficiency at the takeaways but Lily ignored him. It took her a long time to feel affection for Eric and see him as a member of the family, and not just an employee. When they did strike a common bond, however, it proved disastrous.

Gambling is a Chinese tradition and a Chinese curse. My grandfather Kwok Chan tried to make a living hustling at the chess-board in his father's restaurant, then lost himself and his family at the gaming table in Wan Chai. Lily herself never had the time to try it until she was on board the SS *Canton* where small bets added a little spice to a game of mah-jong with friends.

Gambling was actually illegal in Hong Kong, and my father had never had so much as a flutter on a racehorse when he arrived in England. In the 1970s he and Lily discovered casinos, and at this point in the story I have to turn to the tales I've heard here and there from relatives because my father will not talk about that time. I never really knew what happened until I pieced these anecdotes together, as all this happened before I was born.

It began innocently enough, as a fun way to unwind when the

restaurant finally closed for the evening, and it brought Eric and Lily together. The casinos they visited were a far cry from the glamorous gilded rooms of Monte Carlo – there were no men in black tie or stylish ladies with earrings like chandeliers.

They were after-hours gaming halls that consisted of little more than rooms full of hardbacked chairs and plain formica tables lit by glaring halogen lights. Just as restaurants had sprung up to cater for the growing Chinese population, and been joined by boarding houses and wholesalers, so casinos had made the trip over, trailing the diaspora, always ready to relieve them of a little of their hard-earned cash.

They knew their targets. They opened when the restaurants closed and stayed open long into the night. They're still there today, packed with Chinese punters hoping to strike it rich – we all know where they are and what kind of people run them, usually groups affiliated to the Triads. Everyone in the Chinese community in Manchester has a friend or a relative who's in their grip too, hooked on that promise that's always proffered but never kept – an escape from long, back-breaking hours of work and a shortcut to a fortune.

In my parents' day the casinos had a second function, becoming informal social centres for the Chinese community to come together, talk shop and do business. The casinos were like clubs, a place where people knew your name and were happy to see you. Of course they were – every punter meant more takings for the bosses.

When a new casino opened, word got round the community and people started to look forward to the occasion as though it were a ball or a party. The owners couldn't advertise so they gave away free food and drink, and they always, always guaranteed that some lucky gambler won big on the first night. Then the community would really take interest, and the customers would come flooding in.

They were astute about picking the big prize – a red sports car was the favourite gimmick. Red for luck, of course. Whoever landed that would be the talk of the town as he drove around proudly in his new motor telling all the restaurateurs and takeaway owners where he'd won it. He'd be back at the tables in no time, bringing his friends with him, all of them with visions of sports cars and heaps of plastic chips dancing in their heads. The casino owners would win back the money they'd invested in the sports car in no time, and they'd earn enough to buy themselves a fleet of them.

Lily and Eric were snared by one particular new casino that built up quite a buzz after its opening night. There hadn't been just one big win, but a whole series of them, and when Lily went to the wholesalers she heard all about it. She'd become quite an established figure in Chinatown and she thought she should be there to see what was so great about the new place.

One night after the last dish had been washed and Lung Fung packed up for the night, Eric drove Lily and Mabel into Manchester for a big night out. My mother had never gambled before, and Eric and Lily had only dabbled in it so they were all inexperienced. Inside the hall the welcome was warm and the atmosphere was fizzing with excitement – people were winning jackpots left, right and centre. After Middleton at closing time, the casino hit them like a shot in the arm.

At first Mabel would only dare to play the slot-machines. The memory of the poverty of her childhood was still fresh in her mind

– she knew the value of money, and how much the mortgage took for the tiny flat. She says she lost £15 that first night, but that it hadn't mattered as the little family had all had a great time.

They went back a second time, and now Mabel won back her £15 and some more on top – nearly £400 all told, a wodge of paper notes that made her laugh out loud when she collected them. She bought herself some smart new clothes and put some more of the cash back into Lung Fung. Eric took her back to the casino the following Friday to gamble the rest of it, promising her that she had a lucky touch.

The casino became a Friday night fixture. They got through the late shift at the restaurant with a kind of impatient good humour, counting the minutes till they could turf out the last diner and seize their coats from the hooks and head out into the night to get their fix. They all worked hard and what were they supposed to do otherwise? Sit around in the pokey little flat and stare at each other?

They'd come home early the next morning, high with success, with a handful of winnings to buoy them through the week till their next outing. Lily began to loosen up a little and feel the weight of decades of slaving away start to lift. She embraced Eric now, really welcoming him into the fold, and finding a little of the sparkle she'd had back in Hong Kong before times got grim. My mother watched happily, glad to see the two people she loved most in the world coming together.

Inevitably the good times did not last for ever, and the casinos began to claw back their pay-outs little by little as Lily and Eric hit a losing streak. Mabel stopped going, preferring to stay at home, but she couldn't stop her husband and her mother from chancing it once a week, chasing that elusive luck.

Now Lily and Eric would be out the door before the dirty plates had even been cleared from the tables at Lung Fung. Week by week they steadily lost all interest in the business, and the casino filled the gap. They didn't just go on Fridays but took other nights out to go and try their fast disappearing luck.

First the money my father had been given to set himself up in England was lost – years of cash scrimped and saved back in Hong Kong, gone in a few hours at the roulette table. There would be days when a whole week's earnings were poured into the casino's gaping coffers, then an entire month's worth vanished. To Lily and Eric, that only meant that they had more to win back.

They were not alone. There were plenty of tales circulating about others who'd started going to the casinos for fun to see friends and ended up losing their livelihoods, their property and even their families – these stories did the rounds just like the stories about the big wins and the streaks of luck. Mabel paid attention.

She had been doing the accounts for the restaurant since her teens and now she could see exactly what was happening. The casinos were sucking the profit and now the lifeblood out of Lily's restaurants. She tried to talk to Lily about it but she wouldn't listen. She couldn't cajole Eric either. Now Eric and Lily stayed at the casino till closing time, racking up set after set of mah-jong, or watching the little plastic ball flip round the roulette wheel. Sometimes they played hands of poker too, but it was no use. They were losing.

Lung Fung was still booming, Lily's chicken curry continued to draw in the customers, regulars still came, new clients turned into regulars. Lily and Eric worked full shifts, drove into Manchester and gambled for hours, drove back, snatched a few hours' sleep then were up and out shopping for ingredients and prepping for lunch.

They drained jugs of coffee to keep their nerves sharp during the day and winged it on adrenalin at night in the casinos. They began to get mood swings that Mabel grew to fear. A win made Lily arrogant and turned Eric into someone she didn't know, a boastful backslapper who bought her extravagant gifts while the business spiralled down the plughole.

When they lost, the depressions could last for days. Eric would not talk. If he did he could fly off into a rage at the slightest thing, blaming every inconvenience for his bad luck. He stood in the kitchen like a zombie, waiting to come alive again in the casino.

Every time she pulled up a chair at the mah-jong table or took a hand in a poker game, Lily haemorrhaged cash. My grandmother was what casino insiders call a 'high roller', a big spender with deep pockets. The same determination that had carried her through her days as an amah, and the early years at Lung Fung, now focused on the conviction that soon her luck would be in and she would have that money back from the casino. When she realised what she was losing, she upped the ante.

When I can persuade my mother to talk to me about this time I can see her cringe. Lily and Eric were oblivious to the fact that the casino always won. The adrenalin told them that they would win big and keep winning, that it was only a matter of time. I can hardly believe how two intelligent people could fall for something so simple, but then I am not a gambler.

As the restaurant's finances became critical, Lily and Eric started to pay attention. Still fixated on the mah-jong table, they realised that they needed a little more liquidity to go on gambling for that big win that was always there in the next game. They borrowed the costs of the weekly market run from money-lenders at first, then they borrowed a little more, using the house and the takeaway business as collateral.

The loan sharks made it easy, of course. There were no forms to fill out and no credit ratings to be calculated, but the interest rates rocketed after a few months and the repayment demands came thick and fast. When a family fell behind, the loan sharks didn't turn to the law and see them formally bankrupted. They milked their new cash cows ruthlessly, and they had no qualms about slicing off a debtor's little finger with a machete or destroying his property. You did not backtrack on your debts. You did not default on your payments. You did not get any extra time. Usually they were Chinese themselves, and that made them no less merciful about exploiting their fellow immigrants.

When Mabel realised that she was pregnant she was filled with mixed emotions. She was having a child with the man she loved, but Eric didn't resemble the man she had married any more, and this new child meant that she had no choice but to remain with this stranger, who seemed to be dragging them both into poverty. I wonder if she knew then that her own mother had felt the same way years before, when she learned that she was expecting Ah Bing.

When Mabel broke the news Lily, even in her gambling obsession, was pleasantly surprised and delighted. To Eric, it was a shock that jolted him out of his stupor. The thought of being a father overrode the adrenalin rushes of the hours in the casino – for the first time in months he saw what he was doing with clarity, and the real meaning of those rising sums of money hit home.

My mother has said that he entered the darkest period of his life then. He caught himself mid-mood swing and realised just how he had been acting to Mabel. He started to untangle the trail of arrears and loans in Lung Fung's books, and he set about dragging himself free from the casinos. He cut off all contact with his gambling friends ruthlessly.

If he bumped into one of them he'd try to shuffle awkwardly through some small talk and leave as quickly as possible without seeming rude. If they asked what had happened, he'd mention the baby, and say that he had a lot to do to prepare the flat.

In reality he was fighting with an addiction, and he did it in the most wrenching way possible, going cold turkey and taking a searching look at himself. He became sullen and withdrawn once more, the lows no longer interspersed by the giddy highs he'd had from winning a little back from the casino. He was ashamed of his own behaviour; sitting alone he'd put his head in his hands and go back over the things he'd done – his boasting, snapping at Mabel, bleeding Lung Fung for cash. He vowed that he would rather die than see this new baby starve. He had not come to England to live like a low-life in Wan Chai, but to build a better life.

In the long hours after Lung Fung's closing time when he sat and tried to come to terms with what he had done, he won his battle. Now, apart from his weekly lottery ticket he has not gambled for nearly 25 years. The man I know as my father would not set foot in a casino, and frequently warned us about gambling. He threatened us with all kinds of dreadful punishments if he caught us in so much as a bookie's shop.

It was impressive, but not enough to save Lung Fung. Lily's gambling addiction ground to a halt too, without Eric to keep her company and share the highs and lows. The day came when Mabel had to sit them both down and explain that they no longer had the money to pay their staff. The loan sharks had to be paid – they couldn't risk the kind of retribution the crooks were sure to deal out in return for their missing interest.

First the takeaways in Bury and Blackburn were sold, then my father's car and most of the furniture and spare kitchen equipment, but it was no good. Lung Fung had to go too. Lily and Mabel wept. All Lily's savings were gone, every sacrifice she'd made had come to nothing, the years in Robinson Road, the time she had spent apart from her children, the exhaustion and isolation of the early days at Lung Fung – all gone. It was lost so easily. What had been the point of all that struggle if it ended here in this bare kitchen in a cold, northern town thousands of miles from home?

Business at Lung Fung was wound up and the building sold. My grandmother felt as though she was sleepwalking through the meetings with the solicitors and the surveyors as they picked over the bones of her short-lived empire. To make matters worse, Eric and Mabel had decided that they wanted their own business, free of Lily's control, and though family relations remained fairly cordial, they were strained by what had happened. Eric blamed Lily in part for the casinos, and my grandmother was hurt and upset to lose her daughter. They went their separate ways. There was a little money left over when the debt was settled with the loan sharks, and Lily took this and set up a new takeaway some ten minutes away from the old restaurant in a rundown area of town.

My grandmother has green fingers. While the little apartment over Lung Fung might have been unkempt, Lily had coaxed a garden from the soil at the back of the house. When she arrived on her own to take possession of the new premises, she unlocked the front door and walked through the grubby, empty rooms that she knew she'd have to scour clean and repaint, and straight to the back door.

She opened it and found herself staring at a cold, grey expanse. The entire yard had been concreted over; nothing could grow there. It was hemmed in and overshadowed by tall brick walls on three sides, and the sooty façade of the house on the fourth. Beyond the back wall was a factory. Standing on the doorstep Lily began to cry.

She was on her own again. She had barely any money; both Arthur and Mabel had left home now, determined to be independent of her. She thought she could feel her muscles ache at the thought of the work she'd have to do: the scrubbing, the sacks of rice to lug from the car, the vegetables to wash under icy water and chop, the long hours standing in the kitchen, the late nights. It would not be so easy to begin at the bottom of the mountain all over again.

Being Lily, she did it though. She christened the takeaway Lung

Fung too, and set about making the phoenix rise from the flames once more. She had her recipes and her tenacity, and her loyal customers. She made the new Lung Fung a success, and though it never rivalled the first restaurant for fame and profit, it was enough to see her through to her retirement at the age of 75 in 1993, and to provide her with a reasonable nest-egg for her old age. She had achieved much; even if she was not head of her own chain of restaurants, she had brought her children to a better life, kept them fed and clothed, and seen that they had an education. She'd fought her way back from ruin and now, just as Leung had explained to her all those years ago, she had built the first foundations for her children and their children's success. Now she passed the baton on to the next generation.

Eric was starting from scratch too, but he wasn't going to take any more risks, so he and Mabel had decided on a takeaway as well. If he opened a fish and chip shop cum takeaway, it would take a third of the investment needed to set up a new restaurant, but the profit margin would be the same.

Until the end of the 1960s there were only Chinese restaurants – sit-down affairs with waiters. When the American fast food chains arrived and cut a swathe through the business, the restaurants had to adapt. Successful establishments like Lung Fung opened takeaway counters in the 1970s, and the smaller eateries shut down overnight and were replaced by a stripped down takeaway with a waiting-room and a menu on the wall.

To my father's mind the business model was perfect – small,

family-owned and run, the overheads at a minimum. He had a chef – himself, and a waitress – my mother, and that was all they needed. He scoured Middleton for a small chip shop, and found one in Mills Hill Road, a 20-minute walk from Lung Fung.

His family in Hong Kong stumped up a small loan to secure the lease and he moved my mother, who was now enormously pregnant, into the apartment above the shop. It was the first time in their marriage that they had had their own space. He rolled up his sleeves and set about making a living for himself, his wife and his first child. The responsibility to both generations of his family, parents and children, was frightening but he didn't have time to consider it.

My mother worked on the menu and drew up lists for weekly market runs. I can only guess how she must have felt about moving from Lung Fung to a corner chippy, but I suppose she knew that anything was better than being bankrupt. At least now Eric was focused on their future, and they had a home for the baby.

The shop is still there on a narrow road of typical Middleton terrace houses. It's where my sisters, brother and I grew up. My mother still works there, but both she and my father have arthritis now and they find the hours too long for their joints. They keep going though, opening the chip shop part-time and staying closed on Friday and Saturday, the busiest days of the week. This baffles the other takeaway owners, but it seems to work for them.

Mabel laughs off suggestions that she should give up, saying she'd go mad just sitting at home looking at Eric all day, but I think there's a little more to it than that. They're both very proud of their shop and the family they built there, and then there are the customers who come back week in and week out like clockwork for their regular order.

Some of those customers have been coming back to our family for food for over 40 years. Wrapped up in Mabel's pregnancy and the aftermath of Eric's gambling addiction, I don't think my parents had stopped to realise just how much affection there was locally for 'Lil's'. My grandmother had built up a huge amount of goodwill in the community, and generations of Middletonians were addicted to her famous chicken curry. The big-hearted loyalty she'd earned now passed to her daughter and her son-in-law.

The locals missed the old Lung Fung, but when they knew that the chip shop would still be serving Lily's chicken curry, they flocked there for hot aluminium trays of the coconutty stew. Mabel and Eric shared Lung Fung's old customers with Lily's new takeaway, and soon they added more of their own. My mother would take their orders and waddle back to the kitchen to call them out to my father. People asked her how the pregnancy was coming along, and turned up with hand-knitted socks 'for the baby' and tiny cardigan sets.

My mother still makes sure the customers are well looked after. When an elderly regular passed away, she sent money for flowers. Every Christmas without fail she would buy wine and chocolates for all her best customers, even when her own funds were low. For my mother it was these people whose money put food on our own table all year round and it was the least we could do to thank them at Christmas.

She started the tradition of making sure that they're kept in curry while she and our father take their annual week-long break too. Every Christmas she cooks up a huge batch and divides it into Tupperware tubs, then hands them out with instructions for heating it up at home. It's become part of the Middleton Christmas preparations –every year you can see great long queues outside the shop as people rush to stock up. People have come from all over the UK to collect their curry, and once someone even made a detour to the shop on a trip over from Spain because they'd heard about the famous chicken curry.

Back in their first year at the takeaway, my parents were wise to invest their energy in their customers – but they couldn't have known just how much goodwill and extra money they'd need. When Mabel went into labour, there was a surprise in store.

Only my sister Lisa had shown up on the last prenatal scan, but I had been hiding behind her, and not even the doctors guessed that Mabel was having twins. My mother gave birth to Lisa in the Royal Oldham Hospital, eight miles away from Manchester on 13 October 1977. I came into the world two minutes later.

My parents were overjoyed and bounced back from the shock of having not one, but two babies to take home. My mother swears that twins were almost easier to care for, because I looked after Lisa and Lisa looked after me. When I cried, Lisa would calm me down by reaching out to comfort me. We shared a bed, then a room and even a desk when we were older and had homework to do. We kept each other company at school and had a twins' sense of intimacy. You can only be that close to someone when you're a twin.

My sister Janet was born two years after us in 1979 and Jimmy appeared in 1981 – and my brother's birth was a true education in

Chinese culture. Lisa and I had got used to being the eldest and therefore the most important children, but when Jimmy came along he became my parents' pride and joy simply because he was a boy. He would carry on the family name, and that was all that mattered.

Even as a four year old I felt the injustice. It still seems extraordinary to me that the Chinese favour one sex over the other so determinedly when women contribute so much work and brainpower to the family's fortunes. Even my mother, who just wanted us all to be happy and fit in with everyone in Middleton, couldn't resist treating him differently.

Boy or girls, we grew up in the family business like our mother, our father and their parents before them – it was a way of life, and we simply didn't know any different. All I knew was that we lived over the shop, ate from the shop and worked in the shop. There was nothing else.

Sunday was our day off, and we spent it either at a Chinese restaurant having a family meal or at another friend's shop so that my parents could talk to their friends about how business was going and how they could improve the takings. They'd come so close to losing everything that they were wary about taking their eyes off work for a second.

It was the cornerstone to everything. Money bought education and opportunities – my father's father wanted his grandchildren to be the first generation to go to university, and my parents threw their weight into moving their own mountain so that my sisters, my brother and I would achieve his dream.

My father in particular was absorbed in work – like Leung

before him, he had a very traditional approach to parenting. His nickname was 'General Tse' though he had never been in the army, and he was something of a disciplinarian when we were young. He believed that men did not look after children, and though he would call us 'his kids' when we brought a good report home from school, we were our mother's children when we misbehaved. We felt as though we were living with a Chinese father and an English mother – he regimented and formal, she kind and caring.

We always sided with our mother in domestic arguments. She was the one who took us to school, did our homework with us, talked about *Cinderella* and *The Wizard of Oz*, and guided us through all the little problems and tantrums that made up everyday life. Dad seldom stopped working long enough to notice what was going on, and when he did he was only interested in talking to us about our heritage.

There was a heavy educational slant to everything he took the time to tell us about, and it was usually delivered in Chinese. My mother would speak to us in English and press us to think English too, but my father would speak to us in Cantonese. He tried to impress on us the value of Chinese culture, and how it had brought us here, and how traditions and folklore were the stuff of our lives too.

We usually replied in English, to his despair, and there was the added problem that his own education in China had been fairly limited, so he had difficulty explaining Confucian ideals to us smart alecks and instead told us scary Triad stories to try to get us interested.

He even enrolled us in Chinese school, which we hated because it was held on Sundays – our only day off. We got cunning though, because Sunday was also our parents' only day off and they'd oversleep if it wasn't for their alarm. We got adept at sneakily changing the time on their bedside clock, and then the whole family would wake up too late for us to race into Manchester for our Chinese lessons. Eventually my father got exasperated and cancelled our subscription there, enrolling us in a local orchestra instead, which we much preferred.

To some more snobby elements of the Chinese community in Manchester, he was making a mistake by letting us off the hook. I remember going to a Chinese New Year party with my mother when I was ten. There was a lady handing out lucky red packets with pocket money in them to all the children, and she tried to talk to me in Mandarin. I didn't understand, and ran to fetch my mother to make her translate.

The lady said something incomprehensible in Mandarin again to Mabel, then turned to me with a superior look on her face and said in a broken English accent, 'We want our children to understand their mother tongue!'

Mandarin is the official language of China. I suppose you could try and describe it as a sort of cross between the Chinese equivalents of the Queen's English and Anglo-Saxon. I spoke my mother tongue all right, but my mother spoke Cantonese – the most widespread language of emigrants from Hong Kong and Guangzhou. Now that I understood what this lady was implying, I stood fuming silently at her, looking to Mabel.

I could tell my mother was also annoyed because she remained silent and polite to a fault. With a taut smile on her face, she said in perfect English, 'Come on Helen, let's get something to eat,' then she whisked me away to the buffet cart.

From day to day we didn't really see ourselves as anything other than kids in the playground at school, though. We were happy to be English children and not think too much about what made us Chinese and what other people thought about that, whether it was a good or bad thing, and my mother at least encouraged that.

I can only remember wishing I was less Chinese once. I had a phase of being mortified that my nose was wider than those of my English friends, and like Amy March in *Little Women* I spent a few sleepless nights with a clothes-peg attached to it in the hope that I would wake the next morning with a sharp and pointy nose like my school friends. It was so uncomfortable that I soon gave up.

Being Chinese caught up with us though, and we learned that we were 'different' the hard way. The first time we took a holiday my father stayed behind to keep the shop going as usual, and my mother whisked the four of us off to Butlins, promising karting and horse riding and crazy golf. We were all totally over-excited on the drive to the camp, chattering non-stop about what we were going to do and which activity we wanted to queue up for first.

We checked into the chalet and my mother let us girls loose on the adventure playground in the care of the supervisor while she took a break. She came to pick us up at 4 p.m., and we went to fetch Jimmy who was in a group for younger children because he was only six. When we got there my poor brother was backed in a corner, surrounded by a gang of boys who were laughing at him and calling him a 'chink', saying he had 'slitty eyes'. The child-minder was nowhere to be seen.

My mother left us at the door and raced over to Jimmy, yelling, 'How dare you say such things!' but the boys turned on her and started screaming swear-words at her before they bottled out and ran off, Mabel chasing after them. Terrified, we stood and watched, with Jimmy sobbing quietly, and eventually she came back to us, her face red and furious. I had never seen her so incensed.

Gathering us up she marched us into the main building, then plonked us in front of the cabaret where we watched a magician saw a lady in half while she found the main office and reported the incident. She really let them have it, 'I have paid all this money for a holiday and all I get is racial abuse. I want to leave today, and I want my money back.' After that, our father came to pick us up. That was the end of our family holidays for a long while.

Today I find it hard to see myself as a victim of racism. I went to my pick of universities, I've met no obstacles in my career, and I can walk through Manchester without having to keep my head down or worry about who's behind me, but the truth is that the nasty affair at Butlins wasn't the only episode of bigotry that my family had to deal with when we were growing up.

One night when I was about 11 we kids had all gone to bed and my mother was working in the shop on her own. A group of teenage boys came in and the atmosphere in the little room turned cold. They demanded several bags of chips, and when my mother told them how much that would be, they laughed and made it clear that they expected to get this meal on the house. Mabel stood her ground and repeated the price. The tallest of the boys lunged over the counter and punched her in the face, slamming her back against the wall of the shop and knocking her out.

Upstairs we heard her scream then fall silent, and jumped out of bed in our pyjamas and ran down to the shop. I'll never forget my fear – she was slumped on the floor, her glasses smashed, out cold. The youths had grabbed the bags from the counter and were swaggering out of the door, popping chips into their mouths and cracking jokes.

My mother wasn't seriously hurt, but it took her months to get over the viciousness of the attack. Middleton was her home, and the place where she had chosen to raise her family. She had many friends here, and she was part of the community, but after that we all felt unsafe on our own in the shop. If it taught us anything worthwhile, it was that we had to work hard and get our family out of this dangerous position.

My father's English wasn't so strong, so he was a ripe target for the Friday night drunks after pub closing time. 'Solly, no banana' was a popular taunt. Mostly the attacks were verbal, but they occurred with monotonous regularity and they were all fuelled by alcohol.

We children were expected to help out in the shop till 10 p.m. then were packed off to bed before the pubs emptied out, but we couldn't sleep easily knowing that our parents were so vulnerable. We'd lie there half awake, listening for trouble, and for many years Lisa and I would climb into bed fully clothed on Friday and Saturday nights so that we were ready to leap out and run down to defend our mother with our hockey sticks if things got nasty.

There was no question of our not working in the shop though, and from a very young age we helped prepare food in the kitchen and ran errands for my father. As soon as we were tall enough to see over the counter, we were wrapping chips and running the till when we'd finished our homework. It might sound tough for a child to do an adult's job, but we saw it as no more than a chore like making your bed in the morning. It had to be done, and no one could skip their turn.

Later we graduated to peeling and slicing mounds of onions which stung our eyes and made us weep, and to paring bucket after bucket of potatoes. When that was done, my father would reward us with a quick cooking lesson in the kitchen, and my sisters, my brother and I watched and learned as he put together his sweet and sour sauce recipe, which we soon knew by heart.

Even when I'd graduated from university and had a full-time job in London, I was expected to come home and help during my holidays. We learned to multi-task early, and to get our schoolwork and our social lives out of the way in time for the Friday tea-time rush, when it seemed like everyone in Middleton decided to treat themselves to a fish supper or a curry.

It wasn't bad being a source of free chips for our school friends either, one way of getting very popular, very fast! Now that I'm looking back as an adult I can appreciate that those hours in the shop gave me a head start in business. It was intensive experience on the shop-floor of a small business, and it showed me just how much commitment and dedication you need to make a success of any size operation.

As I've said before, you cannot separate business and family in Chinese culture, one feeds into the other and they're both dependent on each other. If you have a business you will not starve, and you'll be laying the groundwork for later generations to achieve even more. The trouble is, that extreme focus doesn't match up to the typical English attitude to family, and as I hit my teens I felt increasingly torn between the two worlds.

My English friends didn't understand why I had to work, for a start, but they had no idea about the guilt trips that tied me in to the shop, the 'Help your sisters' and the 'You can't leave your mother on her own' and, killingly, 'Who will pay for these clothes you want if no one wants to work?' My friends partied and went to discos on Friday nights, and I stayed home and scrubbed potatoes.

My parents didn't understand that I would want to do anything like hang out with friends when I could be making my contribution to the family pot, and they didn't feel the need to make things more interesting either. I wasn't allowed to try something more demanding like going through the chip shop's accounts or dreaming up some marketing. I felt like I was English and Chinese, but was missing the best bits of both.

School was good though, and I was always encouraged to study hard. We were the only Chinese family there, but that didn't stop me having friends and doing well. Good grades came easily, and I knew my parents were proud of every 'A' I chalked up – they never told me I shouldn't aim high, even if I was a girl.

After sixth form I became the first person in my family to go to university when I went up to Cambridge. I chose to study law, and

I know my father was, and is, enormously proud of that. The knowledge that one of his children was going to be a lawyer made all the years of hard work worthwhile.

When I graduated both my parents came to the ceremony, driving up in a new red saloon car that my father had bought specially for the occasion. To my fond eyes they looked comically out of place among the spires and gargoyles in the college court-yards, but they couldn't care less. I've never seen my father so close to tears.

Being Chinese in Britain is not problematic. We're seen as hard-working, law-abiding, quiet people who just get on with our lives and pay our taxes. Sometimes we almost feel like an invisible minority that's just dropped off the radar. I hope we can have the best of both worlds – integration into Britain while keeping the Chinese values that underlie all our achievements.

As Chinese women raised in Britain, my sisters and I have had plenty of conversations where we've wondered who we are and how we fit into this country. We've all had moments when we've felt as though we had no real roots to hold us to China or to Britain, leaving us hovering somewhere in between. Unlike our parents, we don't feel drawn to 'return' to China or Hong Kong.

In my mind, I am neither 100 per cent British nor 100 per cent Chinese. When Lisa, Janet and I talk, we all end up agreeing that we are a different breed, British-born Chinese. We've drawn a kind of comfort and confidence in our Chineseness through food, and Sweet Mandarin is the expression of all this, a true labour of love. I still look to my sisters for support and value their advice. It's not unusual to find us sitting around the kitchen table after work, coffee in hand, laughing and sharing stories about the day. Despite the fact that we have all been away to university, and lived and worked in London and Hong Kong independently, I love my home and the closeness of our family life. We are all very different.

I like to think Lisa, Janet and I are three parts of one entity, each contributing our strength to the success of the whole. Though we are all creative by nature, Lisa is the organiser, Janet the socialite and I am the optimist. We make a pretty good team. Although I know that one day, we will all marry and go our separate ways, for now I cherish this time we have together.

When we were teenagers, my sisters, brother and I never stopped to think we might be living out our parents' dreams as well as our own – we were too busy shuttling from school to orchestra practice to the shop, preoccupied with our friends and our exam results – but now that I know more about the four generations of our family, I can see that that's just what we did.

I hope they see us as achieving some of those ambitions that my grandmother had so many decades ago. Lily wanted to walk among the Europeans as a financial, social and intellectual equal. As my sisters, brother and as I passed through university, I believe Lily, Mabel and Eric saw us do just that. The mountain that Leung set out to move in the village outside Guangzhou in the 1920s was gone.

chapter Ten

BUDDHA'S GOLDEN PICNIC BASKET
HONG KONG 2002, GUANGZHOU 2003

'Three humble shoemakers brainstorming will make a great statesman'

三 人 成 虎

W hen I told my family that I been offered a chance to work in Hong Kong for six months, they were delighted. My father had been suggesting that I take a trip there for some time, fretting that I had lost sight of my real heritage. Their enthusiasm spilled over into us all dreaming up the notion that the whole family should travel out to spend a few weeks with me before my work started in earnest.

We put together plans to spin the trip into a rare family holiday, so that the three generations could go back and see where we had all, in a sense, come from. Predictably, the trip soon snowballed into a huge undertaking. My mother booked the flights and Lily began to contact old friends and relatives, while I researched the hotels.

I was glad of the company, to be honest. I was excited about the move but I had never travelled so far from home before, let alone lived on the other side of the world. I also knew how much it meant to my father and mother to take their first long break from work in nearly 20 years. We had to sort a few things out first though – an old problem reared its head.

My father, ever with an eye on the business, asked us kids who was prepared to stay behind to run the chip shop for a few weeks while he was gone. We all looked at him as though he were crazy. We knew he deserved a holiday, but there was no way we were going to sacrifice ours to make it happen and we told him so outright.

My poor father was baffled and even slightly hurt. Eventually I caved in and apologised to him, trying to explain our position. I did not want to ruin the holiday before it had started with a stupid quarrel. He sort of understood, but he still seemed to be startled by the vehemence of our response. I don't think he realises what mixed feelings we have about the chip shop and the fact that we gave up so much of our time to it.

In the end, despite the row, the trip to Hong Kong was one of the best things we have ever done together as a family. For my parents it was a chance to put their lives in perspective. They too could take stock of everything they had built for themselves in their new world, and they found their romantic view of the 'homeland' put to the test. I hoped that they would see that they hadn't so much run from their old lives as run to a new one, creating a life of comfort and prosperity that many Chinese would still dream of.

The person most affected though was my grandmother, Lily. For her, returning to Hong Kong some 40 years after she had first made that momentous decision to leave was a chance to come full circle. In Hong Kong she could make good on old promises and put to rest some demons. For her too, it was a chance to see if she had made the right choices.

The seeds of this book were sown there. It was the time that my sisters and I started to understand truly the long, tough road that led to the chip shop that we all resented so much. We saw what our parents and Lily had left behind, and how that had shaped them when they arrived in the UK. We pieced together the family stories and rumours, and found out much of the truth about the lives of my grandmother and mother, and the way that culinary skill and a love of food ran through it all. For the first time in my life, I would give my family the respect they deserved for their achievements and their ability to survive despite the odds.

We had booked ourselves into the Mandarin Oriental because that was where my father's father worked as a chef. It had taken barely a generation for our family to get from the kitchens to the swanky five-star rooms upstairs, and it made us all a little proud. Arriving late, we went straight to bed to sleep off our jet lag and the next morning we woke to the city in all its bustling, kaleidoscopic glory.

Our first venture out on to the streets brought home the huge gap between our two cultures and countries. My family stood in a line on the pavement, open-mouthed and out of place. My mother was wearing a T-shirt embossed with the words 'I'm lost in Hong Kong' – it summed up how we all felt.

In the air-conditioned chill of the hotel we had been cold in our summer clothes but now we were all sweating, overwhelmed by the thick heat and humidity. My father was sporting a pair of orange Bermuda shorts – his holiday clothes. My brother Jim had bulging calf muscles which his three quarter length shorts left on display and he soon drew a crowd of giggling, pointing girls.

While we looked like competitors in some madman's golf tournament, the Hong Kong residents were petite, impeccably dressed and swept around glued to their mobile phones. The women even wore twin set cardigans, which bemused me, as I sweltered in the waves of heat rising off the tarmac. I couldn't see how anyone could wear anything more than the thinnest clothes in the sticky morning sun.

I felt enormous next to the people around me, like Gulliver, surrounded by the tiny ant-sized inhabitants of a Far Eastern Lilliput. It was clear immediately that while we were ethnically Chinese and to some extent understood the language and food, we were dressed and looked totally different to the native Hong Kong people.

We moved on to the underground where we were hopelessly lost almost straightaway. It was a million miles away from the Tube in London with its clattering, dirty trains and poky dark tunnels. Hong Kong's underground is spotless and efficient, fully air conditioned and stuffed with tea shops and boutiques. It serves as much as a meeting point for friends as a transport system.

We had planned an excursion to the famous Ladies' Market in *Mong Kok*, where there are dozens of stalls with pirated designer handbags, strings of jewelry and fashionable, counterfeit T-shirts, but we had another culture shock before we got there.

We were trying to puzzle out the subway map on the platform and there were two local ladies standing with their backs to us, chatting in Cantonese, so my father asked them if we were waiting in the right place for the train. They turned round and they were Indian. We were almost too dumbfounded to thank them when they told us that yes, we were going to catch the correct train.

In Manchester we were used to the sight of people of all races speaking English, but somehow this turned our preconceptions on their heads. It was both fascinating and gobsmacking to us at the same time.

It set the tone for the rest of the holiday. Lily and my parents had not been back to Hong Kong for over 30 years and they were staggered to discover how much the place had changed. They could hardly recognise the streets where they had once lived. The old colonial shanty town buildings had been demolished and replaced with 60-storey flats. Even the sea between Hong Kong and Kowloon had gradually been filled in and reclaimed for yet more high-rise apartment blocks. The journey to the other side of the harbour, which had taken half an hour in their day, now took just ten minutes. The city had shrunken and grown all at the same time.

During their lowest moments in England, they had dreamt of returning to Hong Kong – my parents even had a vague plan to retire there – but their thoughts quickly died as they found themselves melting in the furious heat of the midday sun and then, without warning, soaked by a torrential tropical downpour. Both my parents ended up with colds and permanent migraine headaches, unable to cope with the climate.

Lily didn't comment much on what it was like to be back in Hong Kong; we didn't see her that first morning as she was away finding her own ghosts. She was the only member of the family not to stay in the Oriental. Instead she was a guest at her daughter's house.

Under the terms of the agreement she had made with Mrs Lee, nearly half a century ago, she had been allowed to keep in touch with Ah Bing. Over the years, Lily had never forgotten her at Christmas or on her birthday; she had sent postcards, letters and small gifts from England. That ruffled red envelope that had caught my eye as a child was just one of the many that they'd exchanged over the years.

She always kept one Christmas card from Ah Bing on display until the next year's one arrived and it took pride of place on the middle of the mantelpiece. From time to time there would be a photograph of Ah Bing and her family too and they were treated with reverence by Lily, who had them framed and placed, not on the mantelpiece along with our family photos, but in her bedroom, beside her bed.

It was easy to see how much my grandmother regretted losing her youngest daughter and how she kept her memory sacred. As telephone communication had become cheaper, the two had talked on the phone frequently, but it couldn't take the place of meeting face to face, nor could they truly address the feelings of love and loss felt by both just by picking up a receiver. They had a lot to talk about now.

Lily was tight-lipped about her hopes for the visit, and she wouldn't yield up much about the hours she spent talking to Ah Bing, but I know she had spent the years they had been apart battling with guilt. She wanted to spend as much time as she could with the daughter she had given away and now there was no way of trying to sidestep the conversations that they must have.

When I called Ah Bing's house one afternoon to ask if Lily was free for dinner that night, I was told that she was having an afternoon nap. The emotional excitement and the weather were catching up with her. It was Ah Bing, my aunt, who spoke with me on the telephone and she started crying almost immediately at the thought of speaking to the niece she had never really known. The feelings of abandonment were still strong in her even after all these years.

Jimmy, Lisa, Janet and I took a different tack to our parents. The longer we were in the city, the more confident we felt and the more we wanted to know, so we ditched our guidebook and headed for the places that Lily had told us about over the years in snatches. We passed through tiny alleyways that had been home to the poor for generations, where people lived in squalor beneath cobbled-together tin roofs and sold clothing, toys and food on the pavement outside. Everyone knew that these alleyways were scheduled to be torn down to make way for new luxury apartments, making these people homeless.

We took a bus up to Victoria Peak, where Lily had worked half a century before, and looked out over the harbour. The night was cool and the city was laid out before us, strung with lights and the thousands of long neon signs. At a distance it was beautiful and no longer overwhelming.

We had always planned to take Lily back on a trip to her old village near Guangzhou, but now my grandmother vacillated. She had had a wonderful time with Ah Bing but it had left her drained, and, as she confided in me, she wasn't sure if she could handle returning to a place so dogged with memories, good and bad.

On our final Sunday together in the city we gathered all our relatives and friends in Hong Kong for traditional dim sum. It was Lily's eighty-fifth birthday, time for a real reunion. Over 40 people came together around the table for one meal, including Ah Bing and her husband and children. Ah Bing looked so much like Lily that I felt a catch in my throat when I saw her. They both have very distinctive noses with a tip that's slightly turned up and flared – it was strange to see that familiar feature on this stranger and know that she was my mother's sister. The whole family was gathered together, and for one evening we got to feel totally assimilated into Hong Kong life. We toasted Lily proudly.

As I watched my grandmother flushing and acknowledging the cries of '*Gambei*!' I thought about the village outside Guangzhou and what my grandmother must have been like when she left it as a little girl. I wanted to see that place all the more, curious to get to the very beginning of the story. Luckily that meal bolstered Lily's spirits too, and she announced that she wanted to go back to the village after all.

Since the British returned Hong Kong to China in 1997 it has become possible to travel easily from the former colony to the mainland and back for the first time in decades. We crossed into China by train, travelling northwards and back, it seemed, in time. There is an old Chinese saying 'the Heaven is high, the Emperor far away.' I could not get it out of my head as we journeyed through the Chinese countryside to Lily's birthplace.

To me, it explained how the countryside here had been bypassed by regeneration and modernisation. This was the true wonder of the Far East, light years from Hong Kong's hi-tech glamour and skyscrapers. I had never seen anything like the real China before, and now it flashed by the express train. In only a couple of hours we had covered the distance that Leung had crossed and recrossed so many times on the slow, chugging ferry.

The countryside gave way to the suburbs of Guangzhou, now swelled into a monster city the size of London, with air leaden with pollution. We left the train and found our hotel, surrounded by shopping malls and multi-lane highways. From there we took a taxi, and everyone was very quiet, thinking about what we would see and what the village meant to our family. As we cleared the edges of Guangzhou the noise of traffic and the furiously honking horns faded until all we could hear was the engine of the filthy old minibus taxi and the sound of crickets.

Somewhere in the middle of nowhere, the minibus pulled up in a cloud of black diesel smoke and we piled out and wondered where to go next. A few yards away was a dusty concrete bridge which spanned a dry river bed. The driver pointed over it, gabbling in a thick regional accent that only Lily could understand. Lily lead the way and we followed her in the direction he'd indicated, over the bridge.

A gang of children came racing up a dirt road to the bridge, they were wearing only underwear and their skin was caked with dirt, but when they got close they realised we were strangers and screeched to a halt. We hovered awkwardly in our T-shirts, jeans and Nike Shox trainers, feeling as though we were wearing space suits. Only my grandmother was unfazed, and was soon among the children handing out boiled sweets and chatting.

We followed her and her new friends to the village, our feet sinking in the mud as we walked. The cluster of buildings we reached was primitive, none higher than two stories, and their façades were blank concrete. There were no streetlights and no billboards here. We had never seen such a place. Even my mother clung to my grandmother's arms nervously, as though she were a little girl all over again. She was born in Hong Kong, a city child who had never been to her mother's birthplace.

'Follow me,' said my grandmother, quite at home. 'I think it's this way.' We tagged along obediently. No one spoke, but we must have had fear written across our faces. This was quite a different China, far removed from the glossy images of Shanghai, Beijing or even Guangzhou's city glitz.

We were halfway down the only street in the village when a middle-aged woman, dressed half in modern Western clothes and half in traditional Chinese clothes, stepped out of one of the houses and greeted us. She explained that she was our Auntie, and that she'd show us around the village. She and Lily hugged as though they'd only been chatting the day before, which it turned out, they had. Something else that Lily had kept to herself – she'd been doing a little arranging for this journey into her past.

My rusty grasp of Cantonese was now beginning to improve but I still hadn't a hope of understanding what this new Auntie was saying. I smiled at her politely as she chattered on to Lily, leading her on through the houses. Lisa elbowed me and I piped up, 'What is she saying, Pop?' Lily stopped and turned.

'She's asking if I remember this place. I said, not really. I feel like I am familiar with it but it's like a dream.'

I nodded, slightly taken aback by the strangeness of it all, and my grandmother went on, 'She also says that I shouldn't worry as nothing's changed and that Mui is waiting for us.'

With that, Lily turned back to her conversation. We all exchanged glances in shock, then Jim said that if the answers to all my questions were going to be that weird, maybe I should keep quiet. We all nodded in agreement.

The dry, yellow streets of the village were deadly quiet between the crumbling houses. It was incredibly peaceful; there were no cars, no motorbikes or bicycles, no bells, no car horns. A few scrawny chickens and some mangy dogs scavenged between the buildings.

We heard shouts, and as we rounded the corner into the small main square we found all the villagers who were gathered to watch a martial arts competition. At one side, oblivious to the crowd, were two men playing Chinese chequers on a board balanced on a shaky table. Opposite them was an old barber waiting for trade as he sat on a plastic stool in his brown silk pyjamas. The soft whir of a sewing-machine drifted out of one of the houses.

It was picturesque in its own way, but it made me uncomfortable. I assumed that the village was now as developed as it had ever been, so what could it have been like in the 1920s? How had my grandmother survived it? I believed her when she said that nothing had changed – there was nothing to change! My new auntie mentioned that no one farmed for a living any more. During the Cultural Revolution many of the villagers had had what few assets they owned confiscated, and the ancient agricultural system had never really recovered.

On the other side of the square was a dried-up lake, beside which stood a small, traditional temple. We filed in and one after the other took an incense stick to light for our ancestors. Then, with some clicking and creaking, we knelt down on the floor. A tiny, fragile-looking old woman emerged from a door at the back of the temple and shuffled towards Lily.

There were tears in her eyes as she clasped my grandmother's hands and mumbled a few words to her. Lily held her tightly. This elderly lady with her huge, toothy smile and bird-like bones was her younger sister, Mui. Mui had married a university professor from Guangdong and returned to the mainland in the 1950s, ending up in her home village. She had been cut off from her sisters, who had either emigrated or remained in Hong Kong. It pained me to realise that she was half the size of her sisters; she looked older even than Lily, though she was several years her junior.

Still overcome, Mui nodded to us all to go with her, smiling broadly. We retraced our footsteps to a small, low-roofed house on the edge of the square and through the thick cloth curtain that served as a door. We crushed into the tiny house, feeling like giants once again, and blinked as our eyes adjusted to the gloomy interior.

On the wall was a black and white photograph in a cracked frame, weathered by the sun. It was a man with my mother's high cheekbones and dark eyes, and a trace of an expression I'd seen on Lily's face so many times. My grandmother smiled and pointed, 'My father,' she said, simply.

This was Mui's home, and it was the house where my grandmother had been born and had grown up. This was where Leung had planned the soy sauce business, and the place that he and Tai Po had left with their six daughters for Hong Kong in 1925. It was impossible to take it all in. The last 77 years telescoped back into this bare room – Hong Kong, Manchester, Guangzhou all gone in the blink of an eye.

Mui fussed over us, getting her daughter – our new Auntie – to fiddle with the small gas stove in the corner and fix some tea. She was animated and yammering non-stop, and after it had taken her five minutes of song and dance to make sure that we were all seated, Lily started to scold her and Mui immediately calmed down and sat down herself. Half a century later and nothing changes – older sister always knows best, it seems.

Cups of tea were handed round and Mui's wrinkled face cracked into another enormous smile. I smiled back at her, keeping eye contact. I did not know this woman at all. I had not even known that my grandmother had a sister here, and now I could say nothing to her but I still marvelled at her. While the others had escaped, she had returned here and endured poverty, war and the horrors of the Cultural Revolution, and she was still beaming.

We talked all afternoon, even though the conversation was stilted as Lily had to translate for both sides of the family. We learned about Mui's children, and her grandchildren, and what they were all doing. A constant stream of villagers stopped by to take a cup of tea and look over Mui's relatives from England and ask questions. We talked about the weather too, which was ridiculous, but I suppose my family had been in England for too long!

As the evening drew in, Mui took us out to the back of the house to show us her allotment with its homemade greenhouse. She still worked it herself, harvesting baby sweetcorn, carrots, bamboo shoots, *gai lan* and mushrooms. She promised she'd pick out her sweetest sugar-snap peas for our supper.

Back in the house she pulled out a wok which was twice the size of her and poured in a dose of oil. As it heated up and the oil began to spit, she wielded the pan with both hands and went to work. She fried garlic and let the scent fill the room before she tipped in the vegetables, tossing them with a skill born of decades of practice.

As Mui began to cook, Lily stepped up to the wok to help her and now they prepared the dish as if they were dancing together, each knowing perfectly the other's movements as surely as if they had cooked the dish together only yesterday.

Mui added a little clear vegetable stock to the mixture, a pinch of salt and some fresh chives, a dash of soy sauce and a pinch of pepper. Then she poured portions of it into small baskets made of cooked potato and we knew exactly what the dish was – Buddha's Golden Picnic Basket, something that Mabel and Lily had made for us countless times. The sisters must have learned it at their mother's knee and we had never stopped to imagine where it had come from.

Before the meal, the atmosphere in the little hut had been fairly stiff and formal. Over 40 years had passed since the sisters had last met and there was much to say, but it was the act of cooking that broke down the barriers between them. Cooking was a language that spanned all the years when they had been apart, Mui here in the village and Lily in another world in Manchester. The wok united them. As they presented the family favourite to us all, I thought one or other or both of them might shed a tear.

As dinner was served, the house was crowded with locals and family alike, and my father broke out a bottle of plum wine that he'd brought. Having sat in silence for so long, I was desperate to find some way to communicate – I wanted to show that we felt that these generous people were no longer strangers. I proposed a toast.

'Pop, Mui, *Gambei*, Mum, Dad, *Gambei*!' I called out as I filled their glasses with plum wine. 'Lisa, Janet, Jim, *Gambei*!' I cheered. We celebrated life that day, and I hope we paid our respects to the two old ladies. We drank to the future too, and the power of ambition backed by hope. Now I really understood what Lily and Mabel had achieved, and I was inspired to try to make them proud of me.

When we left to take our taxi back to Guangzhou, a crowd gathered to wave us goodbye. Lily waved too – she was staying behind for a few days with her sister. As the taxi pulled away I tried to imagine being separated from my sisters for so long, and failed. It would be unbearable not to be able to share my feelings, my fears or my successes with them. Lily and Mui must have had a lot to catch up on.

The following morning I woke between cool, clean hotel sheets. The village had been an incredible adventure and now here I was back in 'civilization', disoriented and finding it harder than ever before to get a grip on twenty-first century China. My sisters and I opted to stay on in Guangzhou for a few days to try to get more of a feel of the mainland, and see if we could find ourselves there somehow.

We set out to shop for gifts for friends back in the UK, and it wasn't long before we realised that Guangzhou's malls didn't seem to offer anything 'authentically' Chinese. A love affair with Western culture was in full swing, and every shop was stuffed with goods I could have bought at home in Manchester. There were branches of international chain stores too, the same ones you see replicated all around the West. Having seen some of the beauty of the Chinese way of life, I found this hard to understand.

In the plazas of Guangzhou we saw the sons and daughters of China's new wealth and prosperity sitting outside brand-name cafés, eating ice cream and drinking cappuccinos that must have cost as much as a family meal in Lily's home village. I wondered if Western ways were making some inroads into China's food culture, and how the people could let that happen.

Chinese society has allowed itself to develop an inferiority complex in recent years, a revolutionary concept in itself. Though Confucius encouraged learning from others, throughout history China has always turned its nose up at foreign culture and technology. Before the twentieth century China had always been slow to respond to the big global leaps forward, and remained ambivalent about the importance of catching up with the rest of the world, preferring instead to plough its own path.

The recent generations changed all that, showing a real thirst for knowledge and an appetite for evolution. It accelerated at a dangerous and demanding rate with the advent of Communism, and at its height the Cultural Revolution ripped up and destroyed anything 'old' – houses, temples, monuments, and even traditional customs that were dismissed as superstition. All were sacrificed for progress.

When China emerged from Mao's rule, the new leaders realised that they still lagged far behind the other superpowers, and pitched the country into a new breakneck programme of improvement. Mega-cities like Shenzen were created from small fishing villages, without any regard to traditional homes or architecture, and factories and power stations sprouted in profusion. As the leaders would say, if the old does not go, the new cannot arrive.

The urban sprawl of Guangzhou and Hong Kong demonstrated to me how a Chinese city could be as cosmopolitan as any of it Western counterparts, but it was by travelling to my grandmother's hometown in the countryside, where life ebbs and flows as gently as the unfolding green tea-leaves in hot water, that I came to realise that China can also be a place where neighbours stop by to say hello and end up staying for dinner. Hospitality has no bounds. I believe that it is here that the real traditional China can be found.

Against the odds and the terrible threats of the Communist government, much of that old China has survived, and my 85-year-old grandmother can return there and still feel at home. Even most of the traditions suppressed during the Cultural Revolution have emerged unscathed. Feng shui masters still choose wedding dates as they did for Leung and Tai Po. At New Year people fill the sky with fireworks to ward off evil spirits and they eat *lap cheong* sausage. Across Fujian and Guangdong provinces, young people still carry on the tradition of simple tea ceremonies, swirling their tea-leaves like Fat Chow in his restaurant on the Pearl River.

As we made our way round twenty-first century Guangzhou my sisters and I had begun to wonder if there was anything of traditional China left in the city, when we caught sight of some food stalls. We were so hungry after a day of trudging and shopping that we raced over. The stalls looked modern enough, with their red and white striped awnings, and electric lights like a booth at a fairground in England.

We walked along the counters, admiring the pyramids of fruit fritters, the heaped-up shellfish and the balls of dim sum. There were trays of meat and fish flesh kebabbed on wooden skewers too. As I leant in to get a closer look, one of the cooks, immaculate in his chef's whites, picked up a stick and shook it under my nose.

'Snake,' he called. 'You like snake, lady?'

All I could see was a snake on a stick coming at me and I jumped away with a squeal. The Chinese chefs laughed and I glanced at the labels on the stall. I hadn't realised that the stall was indeed selling snake – peeled, cooked and presented like a kebab. I declined.

The locals were not so squeamish. My sister pointed out an amorous Chinese couple sitting on a bench next to us. They each held a couple of skewers and were feeding one another, the way lovers do, with crispy fried crickets. They murmured, giggled, and made eyes at one another and brushed away the stray crickets' legs from the corner of each other's mouths. Lisa stared at them in horror.

We turned back to the stall and made a mental inventory of

what they were selling. Four skewered bats, anybody? Four frogs? Four mice? There were larvae, sea slugs, sea cucumbers, and several other mysterious things that I preferred not to investigate too closely. No greasy hamburgers or döner kebabs here, thank you very much. When it comes to food, the old China still reigns.

After all, the Chinese, I was quick to remind myself, have enjoyed 5000 years of civilisation. They were the first to invent many things that we now take for granted, and they have an amazing cuisine – who am I to criticise their taste in protein? I reckon they know what they're doing, but all the same I bought a pineapple fritter for myself, and felt very English.

Chapter Eleven

SWEET MANDARIN

MANCHESTER 2003–

'Each generation will reap what the former generation has sown'

前人栽树 后人乘凉

It was when I returned from Hong Kong six months later that
Lisa, Janet and I started to plan our restaurant in earnest. We'd
always talked about going into business together, and even though
we'd taken separate paths professionally, it was always with the
notion that we'd use that chance to learn skills we could use for our
restaurant. The trip gave us the impetus we needed, and it gave us
plenty of food for thought.

We were sitting round the kitchen table in my parents' house in
Middleton after another huge meal of claypot chicken and jasmine
rice, with Lisa cracking jokes about old times in the takeaway and
how we used to play hide and seek under the counter, when it
struck us that, well, we were ready. There was nothing stopping us
from getting our dream underway.

We had the capital now that we were in our late twenties,
having carefully put aside or invested our salaries. We also had the

experience – after all, hadn't we been working in the catering trade since we were children? My sisters and I were able to cook our way through the entire menu at the takeaway by the age of 11, and we often preferred cooking to playing outside. We could handle a wok and we could train chefs of our own now. We'd just been reminiscing about the way we got told off at school for making stir-fry when we should have been cooking apple pies. That was the kernel of it – the stories we shared and the know-how. I could see just how we would make it all work.

Lisa, Janet and I were agreed about two things. Firstly, if we argued about money or about who was in charge, the whole project was null and void. It wasn't worth risking our friendship as sisters. We already trusted one another implicitly, and knew that all we each wanted was to do our best together, and not waste our time on something half-hearted and lacklustre.

Secondly, we were determined that we had to create a restaurant which expressed what we were – British-born Chinese in the twenty-first century – and where we'd come from. We were passionate about the food that was our culture and our family inheritance, and we wanted to do it justice. We wanted people to look at it with fresh eyes and taste it with a fresh palate.

For years Chinese cuisine had been synonymous with cheap takeaways and ladles of MSG-heavy glop or 'instant' stir-fries from jars on the supermarket shelf. The dishes that were part of the fabric of our family were nothing to do with that. In honour of the women who gave us a chance in the world we wanted to serve Lily Kwok's Chicken Curry, Mabel's Claypot Chicken and Buddha's

Golden Picnic Basket. They'd be introduced to a whole new generation and their recipes would be passed on in turn.

In Hong Kong we'd seen restaurants that were a million miles away from the classic high street Chinese establishments in the UK – they were sophisticated and contemporary, bang up to date. Sweet Mandarin had to be a mixture of old and new – we'd build on my parents and my grandmother's groundwork, and that of the first great wave of Chinese restaurateurs in Britain. They gave us a chance to be far more ambitious than they could ever have dreamed of being.

We had a lot to prove. Our parents and Lily weren't pleased at first. Why had they done such back-breaking work for so long, seen us go to university and get good degrees, then move effortlessly into professional careers, only for us to junk it all in and go back into catering? I think they were also a little sceptical, thinking that we weren't tough enough to do it, that we had somehow underestimated how hard it would be. They tried to talk us out of it, and it wasn't until we secured the freehold on the restaurant that they began to take us seriously – that's when they threw themselves behind us.

We got to work. Lisa sold her recruitment consultancy in London and moved to Manchester, where she became the mainstay of Sweet Mandarin. She made it her mission to push me and Janet to be more adventurous, making the restaurant a more formidable undertaking and ramping up the number of new dishes on the menu.

I remained in my job, but ploughed my spare time into handling our finances – raising money, making the most of our resources and keeping our taxes up to date. Like my mother at

Lung Fung I was going to balance the books. I also handled our marketing strategy in the early days. When Lily opened Lung Fung she didn't advertise or try and get coverage in the local papers, just kept her prices reasonable and her cooking good.

While we took her basic principles to heart, we were competing in a completely different marketplace to 1950s' Middleton. Manchester is a big, prosperous city where people can eat their pick of cuisines from all over the world. In order to make an impact we had to make sure the restaurant had a high profile from the start, and kept on pulling in new punters to try the menu. I drew up scores of ideas – wine-tasting, services for corporate catering, special menus and themed days. We even organised a Miss Asia Babe contest with a local modelling agency, offering the runners-up jobs as waiters and waitresses in the restaurant.

Janet left her career as an electronics engineer and marshalled her legions of friends into action. They hit the town, browsing bars and sampling the atmosphere in restaurants, before reporting back to Janet with hundreds of ideas about what we should try and what we should avoid with Sweet Mandarin. Janet was going to take over all the front of house business, greeting diners and making sure they were well-looked after.

She was the one who knew we'd found the right location, and badgered Lisa and I into getting through all the heaps of paperwork to complete the purchase on the freehold. We chose a bare concrete box, a unit at the bottom of a block of hundreds of apartments in the Northern Quarter of Manchester.

The Northern Quarter sits on the front line of Manchester's urban redevelopment scheme, an area that mixes grubby, rundown curry houses with organic food stores, seedy sex shops and yuppy loft apartments. It's home to the Smithfield fish market where our mother and grandmother had come for decades to pore over the goods and pick out the freshest fish for their customers or their families.

There's a vibrant street life and a bustle that indicates an economy that's on the up, but hasn't yet priced the neighbourhood out of most people's pockets. It was exactly what we wanted. There was no point in opening yet another restaurant in Chinatown – we were trying to do something new, and for that we needed a new place.

Despite sitting plumb in the middle of the High Street, the space had been a car park, abandoned years ago. Now called the Design House, the flats above the restaurant space were home to people on temporary secondment to Manchester for the BBC and Granada TV. We had hundreds of potential customers already, right on our doorstep.

We chose an architect whose work Janet's spies had seen in the best bars in Manchester, and raved about, and in four weeks he transformed the concrete box with its high, grey ceiling into a light box with two walls made of giant panes of glass. Then we used our knowledge of feng shui to plan the interior, because we wanted to give it a certain balance and harmony that would settle our customers' minds and stomachs. I don't know what Tai Po would have made of the giant photograph of blades of grass blown up to the size of trees that we hung on the back wall, but for us it was an expression of perfect *sheng qi* – a vital, active force.

The walls were lined with grooved wooden panels that mirrored the building's stark, Scandinavian finish, and we splashed out on two huge red leather sofas for the waiting area. We would be running a takeaway service too, targeting busy young professionals in the area. We wanted it to be like the original Lung Fung and my parents' takeaway, a place for locals above all – somewhere where they felt they could just pop in for good food.

We still hadn't settled on what to call the restaurant, and because we wanted it to be part of the community, we thought the community should choose the name. We launched a competition in the local papers and on the radio with a cash prize, and several thousand people entered. 'Sweet Mandarin' came out on top. It was perfect.

'Sweet' is Manchester slang for 'good' or 'cool' – there was our British side – and 'Mandarin' summed up the traditional, Chinese side. The winning entrant could never have known that our grandfather had worked in the Mandarin Oriental back in Hong Kong. We commissioned giant copper letters to spell out 'Sweet Mandarin' and the Chinese symbols for 'sweet, sweet' and placed them on the wall perpendicular to the blades of grass. When you peered in through the glass on a dull and rainy Manchester day the letters glowed warmly in the gentle restaurant lights.

I can still remember the thrill I felt on the day we opened – not so much at the street party at night with the lion dancers and the firecrackers, but that morning in October 2005 when we first unlocked the door. The building had been completed the day before after only four short weeks, and we still hadn't seen what the finished result looked like, without the decorators' sheets and the heaps of cardboard boxes and polystyrene pellets.

It was like a thousand Christmas mornings all at once. I pulled the shiny, newly cut keys out of my pocket and turned to Lisa and Janet, 'Ready?' They nodded, and I opened the door, then we linked arms and marched together over the threshold and into our own chapter of the family story.

I was taught a great deal of what it is to be a Chinese woman in the kitchen at my mother and grandmother's sides. Cooking is at the heart of the Chinese family and for a Chinese woman it is at the very core of her identity.

My strongest childhood memories are of the kitchen – the click-click of my mother's heels on the tiled floor, the white clouds of steam billowing out as the wok lid was lifted, the feel of ivory chopsticks, cold to the touch. Schoolwork and a thousand little frustrations and missed Friday night parties evaporated as we sat down to eat.

This is my inheritance, the living part of our family tree, the traditional cooking that my grandmother brought from the home-land and passed down through the generations to me and my sisters. My mother taught us the basics as our birthright.

Mabel always said that a meal in a restaurant opens the taste-buds, but a mother's cuisine widens all the senses, and she taught me the three most important things about cooking: 'Taste with your mind, describe the dish to tantalise the diner', 'Taste with your eyes, presentation is key', and finally, 'When you cook, you are sharing your heart. So cook enthusiastically.' My mother follows this mindset whether she cooks the most delicate and complicated of dishes or makes beans on toast.

We still love helping her cook, especially spring rolls, filling them with bean sprouts and shards of carrots and courgette. We make fried rice with jasmine, beaten egg and a dash of soy sauce, and stuff and shape *won tons* in an intricate bit of family choreography.

She taught us how to shop too, showing us how to have an eye for the freshest vegetables and herbs on a market stall, and watching the butcher attentively as he chooses and slices her fillet steaks. At the fishmonger, she insists that her fish are plucked from the tank still swimming. We share trips to the Chinese supermarket so I can pick her brains about the best brand of a new ingredient to try.

Lily still lives and cooks in the old way. Every Sunday she makes soy sauce chicken, chickens' feet and peanuts, and a soup of fungus and seaweed which looks like it's made of black hair and cobwebs. It horrified us as children, but now we love it.

We can look to Lily's cooking traditions and we can embrace our family's new world too – it's not an impossible tightrope to walk. Unlike some of my contemporaries, I don't try to push my heritage away. China for them is something from the past, something they often find incomprehensible and embarrassing, but I feel that it is my Chinese roots that define me.

I don't wear a Chinese silk *cheong sam* every day and I don't eat Chinese food every night, but, if I listen to my stomach, I am still hungry if I don't eat rice. We all find a place of balance and I can choose how Chinese or how British I want to be. The amount I use of each changes from day to day.

Last Christmas we cooked two turkeys, one British-style with pork and sage stuffing, baby sausages wrapped in bacon, roast potatoes and Brussels sprouts, the other braised in soy sauce and crammed with glutinous rice and mushrooms. Both were delicious.

I no longer wish that my nose was straight or that I was born Caucasian. When I look at my fellow Chinese in the streets, I see that I am not alone and there is a new Chinese identity here in Great Britain, founded on the efforts of immigrants like my grandmother. Her generation came here for better times and their dream has been validated by the lives of their children and grandchildren, who can move freely in their adopted society and take advantage of all it has to offer.

I thank my grandmother for the courage that allowed her to hang on when a weaker person would have given up hope. In my heart, I know that she is a stronger woman than I. Thanks to her our family is still here today, despite all the heartache and destitution they've known in their lives.

The mountain that Leung told Lily about as a child has been levelled to the ground and the road to prosperity built. It's up to my sisters and me to find our own mountain now, and to make good on the tremendous legacy that Lily and Mabel have handed us.

I hope that if we face the kind of obstacles they encountered – the tragedies, the bigotry, the sheer hard work – we are more than equal to the task, and I hope too that we will never have to make the sacrifices that they endured. This book and Sweet Mandarin are for Lily and for Mabel – *gambei*!

Afterword

'A gem is not polished without rubbing, nor a man perfected without trials'

玉不琢 不成器 人不学 不知义

'It isn't the end of the world,' said my mother, tapping a shard of glass from her broom on to the cold marble floor. She sighed and surveyed the carnage around her. 'At least you're all OK, and that's all that matters.'

The restaurant was trashed. Tables had been shoved aside and chairs overturned, the menus and the place-mats that'd we'd carefully laid out just a few hours ago were scattered everywhere. The shelves over the bar were empty – every carefully chosen bottle was gone, from the dark red Snake's Blood liqueur to the Grand Cru Champagne. Wires dangled from the walls from which electronic tills, coffee-makers and telephones had been ripped.

We'd been cleaned out. The thieves had been very thorough. They'd been quick too – it had only taken them a few minutes to strip the place out after they'd put a sledge-hammer through the glass front wall of the restaurant. The police told us that they thought the burglars arrived five minutes after Lisa, Janet and I had locked up for the night. They must have been watching and waiting.

Sweet Mandarin had been full the night before, with queues of customers waiting their turn for a table. The bar had been buzzing, people smiling, waiters rushing back and forth with trays full of crispy duck and Sichuan beef. Now the night air was whistling through the gaping hole in the glass, and my sisters and I huddled together on one of the long red leather sofas in the reception area.

Mabel had brought my grandmother, and now she sat opposite us on the other sofa, imperturbable. Lisa, Janet and I were miserable. It felt as though all the momentum of racing around and slogging away to get the restaurant up and running was punched out of us. It was hard not to take the attack personally.

Lily had been watching us for a while.

'Well girls. What's been going on here?' she asked.

'We've been robbed, Pop,' I said.

'I can see that,' she replied. She stood up and walked quietly across the restaurant, her eyes following the trail of glass fragments and trampled menus strewn all over the floor. She turned and came back to the red sofas, sat down beside me and shook her head.

'Sometimes, it is difficult to trust anyone,' she said, her words laced with sadness and experience.

I shrugged, 'I just can't understand it. Why did they choose us? What have we ever done to anyone?'

'If they want to get you, they will,' she replied solemnly. 'They're not interested in how you feel, and you can't change your fate.'

'I don't know how you can be so calm about it.'

'Calm?' she laughed. 'When you get to my age, you'll stop asking why things happen and learn to accept them.'

I looked at my grandmother, and thought about her story – about Leung and Tai Po, and Kwok Chan and her journey to England, about Lung Fung and the way she had picked up the pieces of her life so many times and started all over again, moving mountains. This robbery was just another step in her story, and whether I liked it or not, this story was going to continue through me and my sisters.

'I guess it's just one more thing that's happen to our family, eh Lily?' I said finally. 'Sometimes, I can't work out if we're blessed or cursed.'

'Oh Helen that's easy,' she said. 'We've been blessed! So very blessed.'

This was a little too much for me to take on top of the shock of the burglary and I started to cry. I felt so helpless and stupid. Why had we ever believed that we could run a restaurant on our own? Looking at my mother, bravely clearing up the mess, I cried harder. Lisa and Janet started to sob too, and there we all sat in a row in our overcoats and our scarves, crying our eyes out.

Through my tears, I looked up at Lily, and saw to my surprise that she was weeping too. I nudged Lisa. We were all bawling like schoolgirls. What a sight! What a collection of 'strong women' we were! It was all too ridiculous, and when I caught Lisa's eyes, and she pulled a face at our grandmother, Lily burst into giggles and we all dissolved into uncontrollable laughter.

My mother set her dustpan down on a table and scooped up a handful of serviettes from the counter. She took a seat next to her 87-year-old mother, who was now crying with laughter, and handed us each a napkin to dry our eyes. She smiled – my mother's amazing smile which fills her whole face and makes two perfect dimples in her cheeks – and I knew that Lily was right, it wasn't the end of the world.

'I was also the victim of a robbery like this, you know,' my mother said. We looked at each other in disbelief. This was news to us.

'I didn't know that,' said Janet.

'Why would you? You weren't even born when it happened.' She turned to my grandmother, 'Was she, Pop?' My grandmother nodded. 'Helen and Lisa were only one,' she added.

Folding a napkin into a small square, my mother set about telling us her story in the same lyrical voice she always used to tell us tales about the family.

'Actually, we had just gone to buy you twins a birthday cake. We locked up the shop and drove to the bakers' 15 minutes away. When we returned … they had cleared the entire place.'

'What did they take?' I asked.

'Everything!' she said. 'Even the heavy-duty safe and my passport!'

'These men who robbed you,' mumbled Lily, 'They knew what they were doing.'

'They had been outside for while, but we thought nothing of it,' my mother went on. 'They were wearing boiler suits and pretending to be workmen, but all the time they had really been watching the shop. They took so much and we were gone for maybe half an hour. Can you imagine how shocked we were? The neighbours saw these people but did not even realise what was going on because they looked like real workmen – they even had the cheek to say hello!'

'You did well to wait a year to be born,' said my grandmother, meaning Janet. 'They even stole all the twins' nappies, so how we would have looked after you, I don't know.'

'Mum, we didn't know,' I said.

'Well, life goes on,' she said with a shrug. 'Let's just say I know how upset you must be.' She turned to Lily again, 'You can remember how upset I was, can't you?'

The old woman nodded.

'Yes. How could I forget? You cried for two days!' The old woman let out a wicked chuckle, 'I thought you'd never stop!'

'Yes, well it was unbelievable,' my mother concluded. 'I thought everything was ruined.'

'What did you do?'

'I did exactly what you girls should be doing.'

Lisa, Janet and I exchanged glances and looked dumb. My grandmother sighed and there was a flash of exasperation in her eyes. She shook her head at the daughter who'd produced these hopeless girls, then she laughed again, as though the answer to the riddle was obvious. She threw her hands up in the air.

'Cook food and feed your customers! Open up tomorrow like any other day. Do your business and serve the public. It's what we do.'

'She's right,' said my mother, 'but there's something else you need to do first.'

'What's that?' I asked.

My mother chuckled and pointed behind me.

'Fix your window.'

Acknowledgements

*T*here is a Chinese saying that 'A book holds a house of gold', and this book could not have been written without the help of my super grandmother Lily Kwok, my beautiful mother Mabel and my sisters Lisa and Janet. I also want to give thanks for my dad, who has always been there for us and supported me, and my brother Jim.

Thanks to the team at Ebury Press, especially Hannah MacDonald, Charlotte Cole, Susanna Forrest, Caroline Newbury, David Parrish, Alex Young and Melanie Yarker. To a real gem within the publishing world, thanks Jessica Woollard for your belief in me, your enthusiasm and your efforts. Xinran, thank you for your support and wise words. Finally, I wish to thank Chris Martin for making the manuscript sing.

Thanks must also go to all the schools and universities worldwide who have invited me to speak to the next generation and use the book as part of the curriculum for English and Asian Studies.